The Young
Bilbu

Vernon Coleman

Another collection of memories from the English village of Bilbury.

Note
As usual, the names and details of individuals, animals and establishments, except the Duck and Puddle and Peter Marshall's shop, have been altered to protect the innocent, the guilty and those who aren't quite sure where they stand but would like to think about it for a while before committing themselves (or being committed).

The Author

Vernon Coleman qualified as a doctor and practised as a GP. He is a *Sunday Times* bestselling author who has written over 100 books which have been translated into 25 languages and sold in over 50 countries. His books have sold over two million copies in the UK alone though no one is sure whether two million people each bought one book or one person has a very large bookcase. Vernon Coleman is also a qualified doctor. He and his wife (whose real name is Antoinette) live in Bilbury, Devon, England. Vernon is an accomplished bar billiards player (three times runner up in the Duck and Puddle Christmas competition), a keen but surprisingly dangerous skittles player and an accomplished maker of paper aeroplanes. He once had a certificate proving that he once swam a mile for charity and this may well still be in that box in the attic that contains all those bits of old rubbish which ought to be thrown away but which have managed to hang around until the next spring clean. He was, at some point in the early 1960s, second in the Walsall Boys Golf Championship and was awarded with three brand new golf balls which were wrapped in cellophane and presented in a smart, cardboard box. He claims to be one of the best stone skimmers in North Devon. (Nine bounces are by no means unheard of and he has a personal best of 12 bounces.) He is a long-term member of the Desperate Dan Pie-Eater's Club (vegetarian section) and although he can juggle three balls at once he cannot knit. He can fly a two string kite without mixing up the strings but cannot stand on one leg without toppling over. He can ride a bicycle without holding the handlebars but cannot write a note of music or hum the simplest tune. He has never jumped out of an aeroplane (with or without a parachute) but he has, on several occasions, lit bonfires in the rain and is particularly proud of the fact that he once managed to light one in a snowstorm. He has not yet availed himself of the extensive opportunities apparently offered by social media (he says he is waiting to see if the idea catches on) but notices about important events are pinned on the noticeboard outside Peter Marshall's shop in the village and he has had a website (www.vernoncoleman.com)

since the day after King Alfred burnt the cakes. Entrance to the website is free of charge and there is ample parking space. Visitors to the site are requested to wash their hands before entering and to wipe their feet before leaving. Sadly, there are no advertisements or refreshment facilities. The Author is registered as an Ancient Monument and selected parts of him are Grade II listed.

Vernon Coleman's novels include: *Mrs Caldicot's Cabbage War*, *Mrs Caldicot's Knickerbocker Glory*, *Mrs Caldicot's Easter Parade* and *Mrs Caldicot's Turkish Delight*. All these books are, oddly enough, about a character called Mrs Caldicot. Other novels, which are not about Mrs Caldicot, include: *Mr Henry Mulligan*, *The Truth Kills*, *Second Chance*, *Paris in my Springtime*, *It's Never Too Late*, *The Hotel Doctor*, *My Secret Years with Elvis* and many others. He is also the author of three books under the pen name 'Edward Vernon'. All of these books are available as e-books on Amazon as are the 14 other volumes in 'The Young Country Doctor' series. There is a fairly full list of other books available as eBooks on Vernon Coleman's biography page on Amazon.

The Young Country Doctor series

This is the 15th book in the series and so, if the author has done his sums right, there are probably around fourteen other books describing the Devon village of Bilbury and its inhabitants. All the books in the series are available as e-books on Amazon. A few hardback editions of the first seven books were self-published in modest runs but these are all now out of print. The first few books are sequential but after about the third book you can read them in any order you like without getting into too much of a tangle. Bilbury and its residents are, of course, still firmly and comfortably ensconced in the 1970s and will doubtless remain there indefinitely.

Dedication

To Antoinette: You are the point of everything and everything else is merely decoration. Every minute I spend with you is worth a lifetime. Every minute I am away from you lasts a lifetime.

Another Note
Bilbury books now contain a number of 'bits at the back' – in which
I have provided a little more background to some of the memories in
the book. I have described these extra pieces as appendices since that
seems suitably medical.

Foreword

Welcome to Bilbury!

Whether you are a resident, a regular visitor or someone wandering into the village for the first time I bid you welcome and thank you for sharing my life and my memories.

Kind readers sometimes ask if the Bilbury stories are real. It's a fair and reasonable question and one which I have asked myself more than once.

There is one thing we can agree on: there is no village with the name of Bilbury. No real village with that name exists. We know this because if we look up 'Bilbury' in a Gazetteer or a map of Devon, we won't find it. We will end up in a place called Bibury, which is in Gloucestershire and has nothing to do with Bilbury, or we will end up with a reference to one of the Bilbury books which means that we have ended up back where we started and are absolutely no further forward.

So, that much we know: the name 'Bilbury' is fake.

I admit it: I made it up.

But that doesn't mean that the village doesn't exist. It just means that if it does exist then it must be called something else.

And you have to make your own mind up about just how true the memories are and, indeed, whether I exist or am a figment of my own imagination.

My only hope is that you will enjoy reading these memories. After all, that's what really matters. Isn't it?

Vernon Coleman, Bilbury,
Autumn 2018

The Bucket Lists

It is widely believed that the idea of making a list of things to do before you die is something new. It is known colloquially as preparing a 'bucket list' (as in making a list of things to do before you 'kick the bucket').

The idea isn't new.

Not many notions in life are brand new – and this one certainly isn't.

I have a suspicion that if I spent a few days studying the Greek classics I would probably find evidence that the Greeks were aware of the idea. And I daresay that some 16th century gentleman had a little bucket list of his own tucked away safely inside his doublet or stuffed unceremoniously down his hose.

But in modern times the idea was first introduced into the public domain by a man called Sir Hilary Blood.

Sir Hilary was a former British diplomat who was, at various times in the 1940s and 1950s, Governor of the Gambia, Governor of Barbados and Governor of Mauritius. He did a lot of governing. And, of all the odd places where the notion of making a 'list of things to do before you die' might have been published, it was in the 1956-57 Winter Annual of a sports magazine called *The Cricketer* that Sir Hilary originally aired his thoughts on what we now call a 'bucket list'.

'I keep a list of things to be done before I die,' wrote Sir Hilary with the unaffected simplicity common among that small group of mid-20th century English gentlemen who managed to keep a straight face while wearing hats with ostrich plumes in them and who were happy governing foreign people in foreign parts.

He may not, of course, have been the first to have the idea.

But, in relatively modern times at least, Sir Hilary appears to have been the first person to put the idea down on paper. So, in my book, he should get the credit.

Everyone's idea of what to put on their list will vary, of course. And to a large extent the contents of each individual's list will depend upon their age, their health, their wealth and their life expectation.

A young, fit, well-off individual may have 'climb Everest', 'ski down a black run', 'drive a car at 150 mph', 'take a boat trip up the Amazon', 'run a mile in under six minutes' and all sorts of other active and expensive activities on their list.

Someone older and very slightly less well-off might be happy with a desire to feed the pigeons at St Mark's Square in Venice, take a boat ride on Loch Ness and have dinner at Maxim's restaurant in Paris.

Someone with severely limited financial resources might be happy with hoping for a bag of chips a bottle of beer and a copy of the evening paper.

And even quite elderly individuals may still harbour hopes; albeit perhaps less dramatic aspirations than those nursed by those who are still young in body as well as in spirit.

For example, I still remember the surprise Mr Thomas Pidgeon gave me just after his 90th birthday.

Mr Pidgeon was an extremely likeable old man, utterly honest and as straight as a die: an old-fashioned gentleman in the real sense of the word. He wasn't a rich man but I had long ago learned that you don't have to have a big house and a lot of money in the bank to be a gentleman. His eyebrows went sharply upwards as they approached the centre of his forehead, with the result that he looked constantly startled, not unpleasantly so, but just startled; as though he had just seen or heard something rather surprising.

'I have had a comfortable life,' he had told me when we first met. 'I always found life too easy so I never tried hard enough. And so now I don't suppose I can complain about never having achieved anything very much. I've always been too careful; I've always been too well behaved. The funny thing is that although I never worried much when I was young, I now worry more than I ever did. I worry about everything, because I know how easily and frequently things can go wrong. If I have to go somewhere I worry whether the taxi will arrive and if the train will be cancelled.'

I remember he shrugged resignedly at this and added: 'So I solved those particular fears by staying at home. These days I don't go anywhere.'

Like most of the people I talked to who were in their 90s or over, Mr Pidgeon had a recipe for his longevity.

Mr Pidgeon's explanation (and implicitly his recommendation) was that he ate a pickled egg every day for his breakfast and a pickled onion before he went to bed.

These days, only individuals who are 100 or over are asked for the secret of their long life but back in the 1970s it was generally considered that anyone aged 90 or over had definitely ventured out of middle age and was entitled to be regarded as 'mature'.

I used to write down some of my favourite explanations for having reached a ripe old age. Here are a few:

a) 'I owe my longevity to smoking. I have been smoking a pipe since I was 21. I find that it settles my nerves.'

b) 'I wouldn't have lived this long without drinking a glass of whisky every day. Whisky kills germs and bad cells.' (I think that by this he meant that it killed cancerous cells. For all I or anyone else knows he could be right.)

c) 'I never drink water.' The old man who offered this piece of advice told me that when Humphrey Bogart and John Huston were making 'The African Queen', most of the crew fell victim to water born infections. Katherine Hepburn was very ill for much of the film-making. However, Humphrey Bogart and John Huston stuck to whisky and avoided the water. Both remained healthy throughout the duration of the shoot on location.

d) 'I have never touched fruit or vegetables.' The elderly lady who told me this insisted that in her opinion both fruit and vegetables were full of poison.

e) 'I have never exercised. Exercise wears out the body.'

f) 'I ate a lot of fat, suet and dripping.' The 97-year-old woman who told me this claimed that plenty of fat would keep out the cold and help fight off infection. Surprisingly, she wasn't at all overweight and at the time her heart was in tip top condition. She died a year short of her 100th birthday. She fell, broke a hip and was taken to hospital in Barnstaple. Unfortunately, she caught a nasty bug in the hospital and never came out.

I'm not sure that I believed any of those recipes for a long life. I've always rather believed that for most of us our longevity (or otherwise) is a result of a mixture of genes and luck.

'I'm sorry to have called you out,' said Mr Pidgeon, when I arrived at his cottage one Monday morning. 'But I've been thinking about things over the weekend and I've decided that I probably haven't got all that long to go, doctor.'

Mr Pidgeon lived in a small two up and two down cottage but because of his joints he never went upstairs. His bed had been moved into the living room downstairs. Everything in the room was old-fashioned. There was a hand-made antimacassar on the back of a faded and lumpy sofa and two more on the matching easy chairs. Two black and white china dogs sat on the mantelpiece and a rather dusty aspidistra plant stood in a large pot in the corner of the room. A lovely little china cat and an old-fashioned, wooden clock with a loud tick sat between the two dogs. The cat, which had green eyes and a lovely smile, had the words 'A Present from Padstow' inscribed in red around the base. There were three old Victorian framed prints on the walls. Two showed women collecting flowers in a sunlit field. The third, which hung over the fireplace on an iron chain, was a religious scene. There was no bathroom upstairs and when Mr Pidgeon washed and cleaned his teeth (possibly not daily activities), he did so in the kitchen sink. His only lavatory was outside, a few yards from the backdoor. At night he used a chamber pot, which he, like many of his generation, called a 'gusunder' – because it went under the bed when it wasn't actually in use.

'Oh, I'm sure you've got a good few years ahead of you,' I assured him.

He looked at me rather sceptically. 'I've never understood why,' he carried on, 'but they say that you should put your affairs in order when you get to my age.'

'Oh, you've got a long time to go yet,' I told him cheerily. 'But if you've sorted things out then it'll doubtless put your mind at rest. Made your will and burnt any documents tying you into the Great Train Robbery – that sort of thing.'

He looked at me, not entirely sure whether or not I was joking, and picked a piece of paper off the small table beside him. He

12

hesitated for a moment and then handed it to me. It was folded in two. I didn't open it but looked at it, slightly puzzled.

'That's it,' he said. 'My affairs. All in order. You can look if you like. I'm not sure what I'm supposed to do with it. It didn't seem right to leave it for my sons to find.'

I opened the piece of paper. It contained the following list of names:

Norbert
Josceline
Cynthia
Kay
Unknown but had dark hair
Sylvia
Sybil
Hilda
Daphne
Evelyn
Melba

'It's just a list of names,' I pointed out, quite unnecessarily.

'It's a list of all my affairs,' he explained. 'I married Sylvia and Melba. I wasn't sure whether or not I should put them down but I included them for completeness.'

I looked at the list, wondering what on earth I was supposed to do with it.

'I tried to put them in order,' said Mr Pidgeon. 'But I'm not sure about Hilda and Daphne.' He thought for a while. 'I think there was an overlap,' he confessed.

'And Norbert?'

'I was at public school. I wasn't sure whether or not to put him down. But I thought the list ought to be complete.'

'Ah.'

'I can't remember the name of the one between Kay and Sylvia. Do you think it matters? I've put her down as 'unknown'.'

'I'm sure it doesn't matter at all,' I said, reassuringly.

'So, what do I do with it now? The list, I mean. I can't leave it for my sons to find. Julian would be shocked and Geoffrey would probably find it terribly disappointing.'

I looked at him. I didn't know his sons well enough to know why they would feel the way Mr Pidgeon expected them to feel.

'Julian is a vicar up in Lancashire,' he explained, before I could ask. 'He's very straight laced and rather uptight. When he was little he always wanted to keep his trousers on when he had a bath. I doubt if he's changed much. And Geoffrey is quite a different kettle of fish; he's a bit of ladies' man. He's been married four times.' He paused, thinking. 'He's been divorced four times too.'

'Aha,' I said, understanding. I refolded the piece of paper and put it back on the little table beside his elbow. The table also contained a whisky decanter, an empty tumbler and a nicely bound hardback copy of Plutarch's *Greek Lives* with what looked like a shopping list being used as a bookmark. 'I think maybe the best thing you can do with it is to burn it.'

'Do you think so?'

'Oh, I do.'

He thought about it for a while. 'Probably for the best,' he agreed, screwing up the list and tossing it in the general direction of the fire burning in the hearth.

'Close,' I said.

I picked the ball of paper off the carpet and threw it into the fire.

'Still,' he said with a fond sigh, 'it was fun writing it out. It brought back some happy memories. That Cynthia was quite a girl. Well, she was more of a woman, really. I was only just out of my teens and she had a daughter older than me. Funny thing was I never fancied the daughter.' He closed his eyes for a moment. 'It was fun remembering it all; all except for that Norbert.' He paused for a while. 'I don't know why I put him on the list.'

I smiled at him but didn't say anything. I was already opening my bag to take out the portable sphygmomanometer I keep in there.

'Still, it's kept me busy and out of mischief for a week,' said Mr Pidgeon. 'It was the last thing I needed to do; the last item on my list.'

'Your list?'

'Things to do.'

'You've done everything?'

'Everything I can do,' he said. 'I don't think it's realistic for me to go swimming with sharks or taking up pole vaulting, do you?'

'Probably wise to leave those for the time being,' I agreed. 'Maybe in another lifetime.'

'So that's pretty well it,' said Mr Pidgeon with a deep sigh.

He sounded tired and rather sad and this worried me.

We all need ambitions, hopes, and items on our personal list of things to do. Too often I have known people give up and die just because they no longer have anything to live for.

'There must be things you still want to do!' I said.

'The problem is that I can't get out much,' he pointed out. 'Even with your pills my damned heart is only working on two cylinders and my joints are so damned rusty that my sweat is brown these days.'

I looked at him, puzzled. 'Your sweat is brown?'

'It's the rust,' he said. 'I must be rusty inside. The rust must be coming out of my body.'

I was so puzzled by this that I asked him to show me. With some difficulty he pulled up his shirt and showed me his vest. It was one of those thick, woollen ones with half sleeves. And, rather to my surprise, he was absolutely correct. A garment which had pretty obviously been white when purchased now had rusty, orange marks on it. Mr Pidgeon did indeed seem to be sweating rust.

'Have you ever seen anything like that?'

I had to admit that I hadn't.

'It's rust, isn't it?'

'It looks like it,' I had to admit.

I really hadn't heard or seen anything like it. It really did look as though there were rust particles in his sweat and it wasn't difficult to see why he thought he was going rusty. If I hadn't known that it was quite impossible I'd have honestly thought he was going rusty.'

'Let me look into it,' I told him. 'I'll see if I can find out what's happening.'

'It's just rust,' said Mr Pidgeon, wearily.

'Let me find out for you.'

I took his blood pressure, checked his heart, examined his ankles and gave him two bottles of pills that I'd brought with me. I was still enjoying the fact that I was allowed to prescribe for my own patients. If I hadn't been able to take Mr Pidgeon his pills, but had had to give him a prescription he would have either had to make his way to the nearest pharmacy (at least five miles away) or try to find someone to make the journey for him.

'Carry on as before, doctor?'

'Exactly as before,' I agreed. 'I'll find out what I can about those rust stains. And I'll pop back as soon as I can find out what it is.'

'It's just rust,' said Mr Pidgeon, glumly. 'At my age it's just another one of those things. I think I'm getting pretty close to my final sell-by date.'

His general air of gloom alarmed me. Too often I'd seen patients go into a rapid decline when they lost any reason for living. We all need something to excite and inspire us.

'What hobbies did you have when you were younger?' I asked him, hoping that I could find something that might trigger a little enthusiasm.

He thought for a moment. 'Nothing much,' he admitted. 'When I was young I played a little football in the winter and some tennis in the summer. And when I got into my sixties I took up bowls. I can't even manage that now.'

'No more sedentary activities? No indoor hobbies?'

'Well, there was that Cynthia,' said Mr Pidgeon. 'I suppose you could call her an indoor hobby – though we did sometimes have a little fun al fresco.' He winked. 'She lived near to a piece of woodland and occasionally we took a rug into the woods.'

I laughed. 'Nothing else? Chess? Bridge? Stamp collecting? Collecting coins? Shells? Old bottles? Bus tickets? Puppets? Postcards? Musical boxes?'

Back in the 1970s, a surprisingly large number of people in Bilbury were keen collectors and I used to learn a great deal from talking to them. Collecting is often surprisingly educational. Moreover, you can be a keen collector without having a deep pocket. I had patients who used to go round all the local auctions picking up treasured items for little more than pennies. In those days it was fairly easy to pick up a box of assorted curios, mixed jewellery or unwanted old books for £1, 50 pence or even 25 pence. Auctioneers would often knock down miscellaneous items for next to nothing just so that they didn't have to arrange for the stuff to be taken into storage.

The fact is that an enthusiasm for collecting things is ingrained within us and long established; men and women were collecting before they started farming and were acquisitive long before they could really spare the time or the energy.

It is no exaggeration to say that collecting stuff was the original preoccupation of the hunter-gatherer; it is a hobby that dates back further than painting on the sides of caves. And as soon as men started to build temples they filled them with the treasures they had acquired.

And, as I have already said, I learned an enormous amount of stuff from patients who collected things. Doctors working in towns and cities rarely have time to sit and listen to their patients. One of the joys of having a rural practice in the 1970s was that I did have the time to listen. I earned a fraction of the salary a city doctor could earn but I always thought I enjoyed my work more and got to know my patients better.

So, for example, it was a patient of mine who collected old pennies who told me that pennies had been first introduced as English currency back in 755, and that pennies were always made of silver except in 1257 when henry III experimented with a solid gold penny. When the price of gold rose most of the solid gold pennies were melted down and it was, apparently, widely believed that only eight examples had survived. My patient had spent much of his life searching for a ninth example of one of these solid gold pennies. He knew darned well that his search would almost certainly be unsuccessful. But he also knew that there was a chance, a small but real chance, that he might be the lucky individual who found the ninth example of Henry III's gold pennies!

Another patient, a retired banker, had a collection of penny black stamps which he had built up over his lifetime. The penny black was, of course, the very first stamp in the world and my patient took great delight in showing me just how many different versions of the stamp there were, and how the different printings could be identified. My patient even had a sheet of unused penny blacks. In those early days, stamps were printed in sheets without perforations and when a customer wanted to buy a stamp, it had to be cut out of the sheet with a pair of scissors. There was no gum on the back of the stamps so the stamp had to be glued onto the letter. (Envelopes weren't used – the letter was folded and sealed with wax before the stamp was stuck on.)

I had one patient who collected plum and cherry stones which had been carved by a 17th century craftsman called Philippe Santa Croce.

And another patient, an elderly lady whose brother had been a cabinet minister, who had a fine collection of rare knives – including one made in 1606 which was a mere two and a half inches long but which had hidden within it 13 incredibly tiny drawers. Inside those tiny drawers were even tinier rolls of parchment upon which the Psalms were inscribed in 21 languages. You really can't get much more esoteric than that.

I learned that people who collect cheese labels are called tyrosemiophils and those who collect cigar labels are known as vitophilists. I even knew a man who collected old tractors. He was terribly proud that his collection included a tractor called a 1903 Ivel, built by an Englishman called Daniel Albone.

It seemed to me that almost everyone in Bilbury had at least one hobby. There certainly weren't many individuals in Bilbury whose lives revolved around the television. (This was largely because there was too much else to do, partly because so much absolutely needed to be done and partly because television reception in North Devon was worse than appalling. On windy or stormy nights our television at Bilbury Grange showed nothing but a lot of white lines and produced nothing but hiss and crackle).

Things were different, I knew, in other parts of the country. My friend William, who was a partner in a large medical practice, told me that there were tower blocks in his part of the West Midlands where there were, every day, hundreds of people sitting, usually alone, staring at television screens. William and I studied together as medical students and he was a GP in a town where he worked in a large, modern practice. Many parents, he told me, used the television set as a sort of electronic babysitter and patients who were sedentary through ill health used to spend their days watching the goggle box in the corner of the room.

Mr Pidgeon thought about my question for a while and then shook his head. 'No, I didn't really have any hobbies or play any indoor games. Mind you, I used to play pontoon when I was in the army during the War. But I was no damned good at it. I was always the sap who lost his money. I was never a lucky fellow. If I'd won the lottery I'd have lost the damned ticket.'

He thought for a little longer.

'I collected cigarette cards,' he said a few moments later. 'I used to have a pretty good collection.'

'I used to collect cigarette cards!' I told him. 'An uncle used to smoke quite heavily and he always gave me the cards in the packs he bought.'

When I was a boy I'd been fascinated by cigarette cards. Towards the end of the 19th century tobacco companies began putting small, collectible cards into packets of cigarettes. The cards were usually made of cardboard but sometimes made of silk. One side of the card would usually have a picture and on the other side there would be information about whatever was pictured. So, for example, if a card had a picture of a film star on one side then on the other side there would be biographical details of that same star.

Some series of cigarette cards provided practical information and advice. So, there were series of cards on gardening and on first aid.

Cigarette cards were a promotional gimmick, produced to create brand loyalty and they were incredibly popular in the early decades of the 20th century. The cards were always part of a set of 25 or 50 cards and the tobacco company hoped that smokers would stick with one brand if they were collecting a particular type of card.

I remembered that my uncle would sometimes smoke cigarettes made by a company called Players and sometimes smoke a brand manufactured by W.D & H.O.Wills. He would switch brands if he wanted to collect a particular type of card.

As it slowly became increasingly clear that cigarette smoking was a major cause of serious illnesses such as cancer and heart disease and clever marketing programmes became unfashionable, so the manufacturers stopped putting cards into their packets of cigarettes. I suppose the companies might have also stopped putting in the cards as collecting began to lose its appeal. New generations were more likely to be interested in pop groups and television programmes than in details of 25 different types of crustacean or 50 different facts about railway equipment.

'What happened to your card collection?' I asked Mr Pidgeon.

I was desperately keen to find something to provide his life with some purpose and meaning.

'I've no idea,' admitted Mr Pidgeon.

'Did you give them away?'

'No, I wouldn't have done that.'

'Did Melba throw them out?' Melba Pidgeon had been his second wife. She had died of cancer about eight or nine years earlier.

'Oh, no, no, she wouldn't have done that. They're probably upstairs somewhere.'

'Do you want me to take a look?'

Mr Pidgeon thought for a moment. 'Do you know, doctor, I wouldn't mind if you did. I seem to remember I had a pretty good collection.'

I found his cigarette collection in an old, green suitcase that had heavy leather corner protectors. It looked like one of the suitcases that were issued to service personnel during the Second World War. Inside the case there were dozens of albums and a tin box full of loose cards. With some difficulty I managed to carry the suitcase downstairs. I placed it on the floor beside him and opened it.

'Ye gods!' said Mr Pidgeon, astonished. 'Quite a collection! Pass me that tin box, would you, doctor?'

I lifted the tin box out of the suitcase and handed it to him. He put it on his lap and opened it. 'I never got round to sorting these!' he said. 'I should do that.'

Before I left I helped him move from his chair to the table and I put the contents of the suitcase on the table.

'This is going to take me forever!' he said. 'I need to sort these out.' He rummaged around and then looked up at me. 'I remember now, I'd started a collection of cards about English customs and traditions. I'd really like to finish what I'd started.'

'Can you still find old cigarette cards?' I asked.

'Oh yes! They come up at auction quite often. I can ask Patchy Fogg to look out for cards for me. And there are still a couple of shops in London selling cigarette cards – they used to send out catalogues. I'll have to find out if they still do. And there's a magazine for cigarette card collectors. I'll have to subscribe to that again.' Patchy Fogg, one of my closest friends and an antique dealer, will always look out for specific items if requested to do so by villagers. Sometimes he charges a small commission but more often than not he doesn't even accept payment for the item he's bought on their behalf.

'It sounds as if you're going to be busy!'

'Oh yes!' he agreed.

When I said 'goodbye' he was so preoccupied with the cigarette cards that he hardly lifted his head.

'Have you ever come across a patient who produces orange sweat?' I asked my friend William that evening. Because his medical practice was fairly close to the medical school where we both trained, he occasionally went to meetings where he met medical researchers, and sometimes he heard of new discoveries and theories which hadn't been described in the medical journals.

'Maybe he's going rusty?' suggested William immediately.

'Too late,' I said. 'The patient got there before you with that theory.'

William apologised. 'Seriously, I've never heard of anything like that.'

I explained exactly what I'd seen. 'The only thing I could think of is that one of the drugs he's taking could be affecting the colour of his secretions.'

'I suppose that's possible,' agreed William. 'I'll have a word with Atholl if you like.'

I said that would be great and asked him to let me know if he came up with any useful information or ideas.

Atholl, an Australian, had trained as an anaesthetist but now worked as a General Practitioner in the practice where William was a partner. More importantly as far as my query was concerned, Atholl's brother, whose name was Dennis, worked as a research biochemist specialising in drug side effects.

In medicine, as in so many other areas of life, finding the answers isn't just a question of knowing what questions to ask, it is also often a question of knowing the right people to whom to put the questions. I gave William the names of the prescription drugs that Mr Pidgeon was taking.

I'd rather expected it to take a few days before I heard anything but I heard back from Will less than 24 hours after we had spoken.

'It's called chromhidrosis,' said Will, the moment I picked up the receiver.

'Chromwhat?'

'Chromhidrosis,' repeated Will. 'Coloured sweat. Hidrosis is Greek for sweating.'

'And chrom is the Greek word for colour?'

21

'Absolutely. Well, I think the word is chroma, but chrom is the root which is used when making up new words.'

'OK, well I'm pleased it's got a name but did Dennis have an explanation for my patient's rusty sweat?'

'He certainly did. It's caused by those damned pills his mad doctor prescribed for him.' Will laughed.

'Which one?'

'You!'

'No, which drug?'

Will told me.

'I've never known anything like this happen before,' I said. 'There's no mention of it in the drug company's information sheet.'

'I know there isn't,' said Will. 'And I've prescribed the same drug hundreds of times without seeing anything like this.' He paused. 'Of course, I suppose it's possible that patients who had rust coloured sweat just didn't mention it. Or maybe they didn't notice it.'

'Did Dennis say how common it is?'

'He said it's rare. And if he says something is rare then it really is rare. In some patients it's apparently caused by a substance called lipofuscin being deposited in the sweat glands but whether that's what happened with your patient is a bit of a mystery. Dennis says he's heard of people producing both red and blue sweat. He said he did hear of a woman in America who produced pink sweat.'

'Had he come across rust coloured sweat before?'

'No, he was quite excited about that. He wondered if you could send him some samples of the sweat and maybe a photo or two. I think he's planning to do a short paper for some obscure medical journal and he's collecting pictures of different coloured sweats.'

I promised that I'd send off what Dennis needed. 'Is it dangerous? Do I need to do anything other than switch the patient's pills? These control his condition very well but I could find something else to give him.'

'Dennis says there is no danger and that if your patient doesn't mind producing coloured sweat there is no need to stop the drug he's taking. There's no treatment other than stopping the drug. All he knows is that it's caused by the drug, it's not a life-threatening condition and it's very rare.'

As soon as I'd finished talking to William, I hurried off round to Mr Pidgeon's home to give him what I thought was good news.

When I got there he was sitting at his dining table, which was covered with piles of cigarette cards. Some of the cards were in albums, some were stacked together in little piles, fastened with rubber bands, and some were loose, spread around and clearly being sorted into categories.

'So I'm not rusty inside?' said Mr Pidgeon. I didn't really get the impression that he was bothered much either way.

'No, you're not. It's just a side effect of one of the drugs you're taking.' I handed him a new bottle of pills. 'I'm going to change your medication and you should stop producing rust coloured sweat in a few days.'

I then retrieved the bottle of pills that had caused the problem and, with Mr Pidgeon's permission took some samples and photographs of his sweat and sweat stained clothes. I popped the bottle of pills, the samples and my camera back into my black medical bag.

'Am I going to be famous?' he asked me, when I explained what the photographs were for.

'I'm afraid not; not really,' I said. 'You won't be identified and the photos will appear in some very obscure journal with no more than a few hundred readers.'

'Oh,' said Mr Pidgeon. For a brief moment he sounded disappointed.

'How are you getting on with all those?' I asked, nodding towards the pile of cigarette cards on the table.

Mr Pidgeon's face lit up. 'I can't believe how much stuff there is here!' he said, proudly.

He showed me sets of cards showing radio stars, film stars and music hall stars, reminding me just how transient fame can be. 'Some of these people are forgotten now,' he said, 'but they were huge stars just a few decades ago. Gracie Fields was the best paid film star in the world in the 1930s, and probably one of the most famous women on the planet, but how many people have heard of her today? Have you heard of Fred Archer, Tom Sayers or Dan Leno?'

I had to confess that I knew the names but couldn't remember what they did or what they were famous for.

'Fred Archer was an English flat race jockey. For a long time he was described as the best jockey the world had ever known. Tom Sayers was a very successful bare knuckle prize fighter. Dan Leno was a music hall comedian and a huge star.' Mr Pidgeon held up a card showing a portrait of Dan Leno. 'And in America, there were Clara Bow, Louise Brooks and Lillian Gish – three of the greatest movie stars of the 1920s. But now they're almost forgotten!'

Mr Pidgeon showed me a set of cards showing the English counties and the industries for which they were famous; cards illustrating and describing famous escapes, paintings, ties and ships' figureheads; a set of cards showing different birds' beaks; a complete collection of cards showing photographs of English seaside resorts; a set describing popular superstitions; a small pile of cards with pictures and biographical details of American baseball players, and sets illustrating traditional London cries and unusual jobs. I picked up one of these latter cards and was astonished to see that before alarm clocks became popularly available, there were women in the capital whose job it was to go around the streets waking up their customers. According to the card I had picked up, one woman used a peashooter and a pocket full of dried peas and used to shoot peas at the windows of her regulars until they opened the window to let her know that they were awake and that she could move on to her next customer.

'These are amazing!' said Mr Pidgeon, his eyes wide open with delight. 'I've got a couple of thousand that need sorting into categories. And then I'm going to try to complete my collection of English customs and traditions. This is going to keep me busy for years!'

I was delighted to see that his old hobby had rejuvenated him.

'I found an old, out-of-date catalogue in with the cards,' he said. 'So I've written off to the company asking them to send me a copy of their latest catalogue.' He picked an envelope up off the table. 'Would you post this for me, please, doctor? I'll give you the money for the stamp.'

I happily took the envelope from him, grinned and told him that I had a supply of stamps at Bilbury Grange.

It was good to see that Mr Pidgeon had been revitalised by rediscovering his old, long-forgotten hobby. He didn't actually say 'I've got a reason to live now' but it wasn't difficult to see that was how he felt. Like Sir Hilary Blood, Mr Pidgeon now had something real on his 'list of things to do before I die'.

This age-old phenomenon was something which I often noticed among my patients.

In particular, I can remember Jack Rutherford and Maisie Peters.

The two weren't related and the only thing they had in common was that they both lived in Bilbury and were both patients of mine.

Both had slightly unusual ambitions on their lists and at first glance it seemed unlikely that they would ever succeed in achieving them. (Though that is not, and should never be, a reason for not having something on your 'to do' list.)

Mr Rutherford was quite young; he was in his late sixties at the time of which I am writing, and he was still quite sprightly. He was still active and played skittles and shove halfpenny at the Duck and Puddle. He had played table tennis for more years than most people could remember. He had been the North Devon champion six times in his lifetime. For most people this would have probably been enough but for Mr Rutherford it was merely frustratingly close to satisfying. His brother, Jeffrey, who had died a year or two earlier, had been the area's table tennis champion seven times and Mr Rutherford's ambition was to equal his brother's record. He didn't want to beat it, he merely wanted to equal it. He definitely didn't want to beat his brother's record; they had been very close. And when he'd equalled his brother's table tennis record, he wanted to win the skittles and shove halfpenny championships. He'd been pretty near to winning those on several occasions. But he would be able to play both those games well into his seventies while for the table tennis his time was running out.

The problem was that for the last two years Mr Rutherford had been beaten in the final by a young man from Combe Martin called Colin Tudgel. And as Mr Rutherford got older and slower, as the inevitabilities of age took their toll, so the much more agile Mr Tudgel gained in experience and got faster and increasingly adept. It really looked as though Mr Rutherford was never going to match his brother's record.

'I'd happily retire from table tennis and concentrate on skittles and darts,' said Mr Rutherford. 'If only I could just get that one more win to match Jeffrey.'

Mr Rutherford was the oldest member of a large family. He and his wife Elsie lived in a cottage in Bilbury which had the most beautiful and colourful small cottage garden. It was one of those traditional English cottage gardens which are so crammed with flowers that there is literally no room for weeds to grow.

When I first came to live in Bilbury, I assumed that the flowers in a cottage garden were there simply for their beauty but over the years I learned that the flowers were originally planted not so much for their beauty as for their usefulness.

Most of the popular flowers traditionally associated with a cottage garden were thought to have medicinal or culinary uses and though there is still no scientific evidence supporting many of the traditional beliefs, you'd have to be brave to bet against the popular plants having real value. After all, digitalis, still the most valued drug in the treatment of heart trouble, is derived from the foxglove plant.

Marigolds could be used to add colour to butter and cheese; the leaves and flowers of pansies and violas were regarded as rich in vitamins A and C and were used to flavour honey and garnish salads; cowslip flowers and roots were used to treat blocked noses and throats and for bronchitis, for headaches and muscle problems; mignonette was used both as a laxative and as a diuretic; the hollyhock plant was used for breathing problems and for digestive troubles and some claimed that applying the hollyhock directly to the skin could help heal inflammation; the oil from lavender was believed to be an antiseptic and an anti-inflammatory and was used in the treatment of pains and digestive problems; lily of the valley was used to treat strokes, heart irregularities and urinary tract infections and Sweet William was used as a relaxant. And of course, parsley, sage, rosemary, thyme and many other herbs were used both for cooking and for medicinal purposes.

In the days before medicine became something approaching a science, the cottage garden was far more than just pleasing to the eye; it was the householder's private pharmacy.

I wouldn't swap my modern pharmacy for these traditional remedies, and I wouldn't recommend any of these floral cures, but there is no doubt that for many years the cottage garden was more than just a treat for the eyes.

Although Mr and Mrs Rutherford lived in our village, their three children, two sons and one daughter, all lived in or around

Barnstaple. The Rutherfords had a total of eight grandchildren, the oldest of whom was twenty and the youngest was still not at school.

The parents of the three youngest grandchildren had taken to giving their children names according to where they had been conceived.

'I think they got the idea off the television,' said Mrs Elsie Rutherford. 'I gather it's fashionable for celebrities to call their children after the place where their parents think they were conceived. So you get all these children called 'Paris', 'Rome', 'London', 'Brooklyn' and 'Dallas'.'

'I've heard of it happening,' I agreed. I confess that it had always seemed to me to be a pretty cruel thing to do. What child wants to be constantly reminded of their intimate origins?

'Well, it seems a bit daft to me when you've never been further south than South Molton, further north than Combe Martin, further east than Taunton and further west than Bideford!' said Mrs Rutherford. 'I've got one grandchild called Barbrook, one called Patchole and one unfortunate granddaughter who is going to have to go through life known as Tattiscombe – you can tell what she's going to be called when she starts school!' She laughed. 'George and Jenny seem to be keen on making love al fresco and we live in fear that they'll start a baby in Mattock's Down, West Burford or Little Witton.'

Fortunately, Mrs Rutherford's other two children had been more traditional in naming their offspring.

The oldest grandchild, a girl, was called Fiona and she was single. She worked as a waitress in a café in Ilfracombe and although I didn't know her, Mrs Rutherford had told me that she was very popular with the male customers. 'She's very well shaped,' said Mrs Rutherford, explaining this with a simple movement with her hands. 'And she's not shy. Her boss is very fond of her because she always dresses to please the customers.'

'Are the family coming to the North Devon table tennis final?' I asked Mrs Rutherford, when she came in for her monthly weighing. She had been slowly losing weight for two years and having lost four stone she was now down to 12 stone. The final was, as usual, being held in the skittle room at the Duck and Puddle. Because Bilbury had one of the finalists and because it was pretty well-known that Mr

Rutherford was desperate to win, it was an event causing much interest in the village.

'Oh we'll all be there,' said Mrs Rutherford. 'Except for our Fiona – I don't think she'll be there. It's a bit embarrassing really because she's set her cap at that Colin Jones, the chap her grandfather will be playing in the final. She won't be there because she knows how much her Granddad wants to win. She's a bit torn you see.'

'I bet it would help her Granddad if she did turn up,' I said. 'Try to persuade her to be there – especially if she sits right at the front where she can be clearly seen.'

The table tennis tournament final was being held in the skittle alley, the only room at the Duck and Puddle that was big enough to hold a table tennis table together with fifty or sixty spectators, while ensuring that the players had room to move about freely. The spectators at the front sat down on chairs or wooden benches so that the spectators behind them could look over their shoulders and watch what was happening.

'You mean that if Fiona sat there making cow eyes at him she might distract that young Colin?'

'It did occur to me. Colin will have plenty of chances to win in the future – especially if your husband wins this one last tournament and retires.'

'I'll have a word with her,' said Mrs Rutherford, with a wink.

Things turned out even better than the two of us had dared hope.

Young Fiona Rutherford turned up in a low cut dress that was so short that it was only just on the legal side of decent. It occurred to me that I could have given her a pretty comprehensive medical examination without her removing it.

'I don't think I've ever seen a cleavage quite that deep,' said 'Harry' Stottle, the former Dr Pelham Ronald Eckersley of London, now known semi-officially as Gengolphus Stottle and informally known as Harry. Now employed as the barman at the Duck and Puddle, Harry who had constructed a close alliance with a young woman who earned her living taking off her clothes, was a man who considered himself something of an expert on such matters. 'If you yodelled into that cleavage you would have to wait a day and a half for the echo to bounce back.'

Fiona, who had been invited to the tournament ostensibly to give her grandfather support, was clearly so keen to attract the attention of Colin, the other finalist, that she smiled at him constantly. Whenever possible she picked up the ball and handed it back to him. This, inevitably, always seemed to entail a good deal of bending forwards and giggling.

It was really no surprise when Mr Rutherford won the tournament, received a seventh small trophy (to put into the bookcase with the other six) and duly retired.

Colin Jones, who had something of a reputation as a bad loser, was surprisingly good natured in defeat when Fiona generously agreed to allow him to take her to the cinema the following Friday. It was clear that Mr Jones's prize was not the sort that would fit into a bookcase.

'I don't know what was wrong with young Colin this evening,' said Mr Rutherford afterwards. 'He didn't seem to be playing as well as I've seen him play. He missed a lot of easy shots.' He sighed, accepting a complimentary pint of Old Restoration handed to him by Frank. 'Still, I'm not grumbling.' I don't think I'd ever seen him quite so happy. 'Now that I've got that out of the way I can concentrate on my darts and my skittles!'

There was no doubt that Mr Rutherford still had plenty to live for and that removing that last driving ambition had been good for him.

'That was an excellent idea of yours, doctor!' whispered Mrs Rutherford afterwards. 'I think everyone's going home happy tonight.' She took hold of my wrist and squeezed tightly. 'It means a lot to him,' she added in a voice that was trembling. I looked down at her. There were tears in her eyes. With her other hand she took a handkerchief out of her handbag and dabbed at her eyes. 'Silly me,' she said to no one in particular. 'What will you think of me?' I put my arm around her and hugged her. I had to make quite an effort to ensure that there were no tears in my eyes.

At 92-years-old (or, as she preferred to put it, 92 years young) Maisie Peters may have looked old, and she was certainly frail, but she still had a sharp mind, an excellent memory and a rather wicked sense of humour.

A bishop's daughter, and the widow of a clergyman who had looked after a rural parish in Cornwall, she had lived in Bilbury since the death of her husband around 15 years earlier.

When Mrs Peters spoke to me it was always in the manner I had previously associated with a certain Miss Hwfa (pronounced Hoofa) Dervish, a primary school teacher of some certain years, who had been given the responsibility of supervising a good part of my early education, and who had, I remembered, taken the responsibility exceedingly seriously. She always spoke as though I were guilty of some heinous crime. Mrs Peters reminded me of Miss Dervish, though there was an impishness about Mrs Peters that I was never aware of when Miss Dervish was talking. When not in her classroom, Miss Dervish had always worn a hat with, it appeared, more flowers than could be seen in any cemetery, even after a big funeral. I'm not sure how I knew but I instinctively felt that Mrs Peters would have never worn such a hat. She had far too well-developed a sense of humour to have worn anything quite so comical.

Decades before, Mrs Peters's father had been a famous climber. He was one of the few men to have climbed both the west face of the Eiger and the Matterhorn and Mont Blanc. I remember her once telling me that he had, 'of course, climbed the west face of the Eiger, since the north face had not been conquered until 1938'. I suspect that by 1938 her father's climbing days had long been over. Mrs Peters once told me that although her father had never injured himself while climbing, he had broken a leg while ascending a rather rickety set of wooden steps to a pulpit in Barnsley.

Mrs Peters and her late husband had lived in a vicarage provided by the church and when the Reverend Peters had, as she put it, 'headed upstairs to meet the Boss', she'd had to leave the vicarage.

She'd come to Bilbury more by accident than design.

She'd been on holiday in Lynmouth, just along the coast, when she had seen an advertisement for Spider's Web Cottage in the window of an estate agency in the neighbouring village of Lynton. The cottage had been in a village she'd never heard of – Bilbury.

I don't think I will ever forget the first time I met Mrs Peters.

She'd had a bad attack of influenza and was lying in bed, alternately coughing and sneezing. She had the beginnings of pneumonia and I had tried to persuade her to let me send her into the small cottage hospital we ran in Bilbury. (Our hospital, in the home of Dr Brownlow, my predecessor, was official known as the Brownlow Country Hotel in order to avoid a variety of unbearably strict regulations which would have required us to build up an impossibly expensive administrative structure, but it was run most efficiently by Dr Brownlow's former butler and a number of caring volunteers, many of whom were themselves well into their 80s.) But Mrs Peters was adamant that she wanted to stay at home.

'I'm sure your hospital is an excellent place,' she said, 'but I'll be far more comfortable here, thank you, doctor,' she said. 'And if I'm going to die then I want to die in my own bed, thank you very much. I've got all my books here, and my wireless.' She pointed to an overladen bookcase in her bedroom and to an old, wooden wireless set which was on a bedside table within easy reach. The back of the set had been lost and the valves were now quite visible. 'All the greats have been on that wireless,' she said with some pride. 'That old set has heard them all.' She looked at it admiringly. 'All the great comedians have been on it. I've listened to 'ITMA', 'The Goons', 'Hancock's Half Hour', 'Educating Archie' and 'The Navy Lark' on that set. And the great singers too – Gracie Fields, George Formby and Vera Lynn – they've all sung on that old wireless. And the wonderful concerts I've enjoyed! Goodness, I wonder how many of those Promenade concerts I've listened to over the years.'

And in the end I had, of course, given in and let her stay at home, in her own bed.

'You probably think I'm old,' she said, rather firmly. 'But when I reached 70 I decided that however many birthdays I had, old age would always be a good ten years older than me. So as far as I am concerned, I am now just firmly established in my middle years and although old age is always approaching, I will never quite reach it. You have to remember, young man, that ageing is the only available way to live a long life.'

She made me laugh a good deal.

'I have no time to grow old,' she once said. 'Shakespeare wrote about the elderly being sans teeth, sans eyes, sans taste and sans everything but I am not sans anything.'

Tucked into the mirror in her bedroom she had a postcard upon which was written this quote from Cicero: 'It is not by muscle, speed or physical dexterity that great things are achieved, but by reflection, force of character and judgement; in these qualities old age is usually not poorer but richer.'

Later, when she was recovered from her chest infection, she told me that she remembered that in his later years her father's great joy had been reading the obituary page in *The Times* newspaper. 'He was constantly looking to see who had died and how old they were when they had gone. When he spotted that someone five years younger than him had died he was full of beans for the whole day; as though he had just won some sort of competition.' She added that her father also tried to keep up with the health of everyone he knew. "He won't last long,' he would say with relish. 'He can't have more than three months to last. I can beat that easily.'' She laughed uproariously when she told me all this.

When she was ill I promised that I would call in every day and I arranged for a couple of neighbours to sit with her when they could, to take in meals, change her bed linen and help her to and from the bathroom.

On the second day of her illness I noticed when I visited her that there was a piece of string tied to one of the posts of her iron bedstead. The other end of the string appeared to disappear through the window. When I asked Mrs Peters what the string was for she gave it a sharp tug and outside I could hear what sounded like the clatter of a great number of tin cans.

'What on earth...?'

Mrs Peters tried to laugh but started to cough. I handed her a glass of water and waited for the coughing to stop.

'The other end of the string is tied to a pile of old cans,' she explained. 'It's to scare off the birds.'

She explained that she loved seeing and hearing the birds but that she objected to them stealing all the fruit on her cherry tree.

'When I see the birds in the tree I just pull my bit of string and frighten them off,' she explained. 'There are bird feeders by the back door so they can help themselves to seeds and nuts. A kind young man put them up for me and he fixed up the string and the tin cans.'

'Who was that?' I asked.

'His name is Mr Robinson,' she said. 'Do you know him?'

'Oh yes,' I said. 'I know Thumper Robinson very well.'

'He seems a nice young man,' she said. 'I don't know how he heard I was poorly. But he came and offered to do my shopping for me.'

I didn't know he'd heard. I hadn't mentioned Mrs Peters to him. But I wasn't surprised. Thumper knew just about everything that was going on in the village and he was always ready to do what he could to make life easier for older villagers. I always felt (and still do) that he was the sort of person who really should have appeared on the Queen's honours lists instead of politicians and pop stars.

'Does Mr Robinson have a bad leg?' she asked.

'No, why do you ask?'

'When I was out in the village I saw him from his truck and he seemed to be limping.'

'Ah,' I said. 'If I tell you why then you must keep it to yourself.'

'Of course I will.'

I explained that Thumper occasionally appeared to walk with a stiff leg because he carried a gun inside his trousers.

'Goodness gracious! Is he a gangster? Does he rob banks?' asked Mrs Peters. She sounded more excited than critical.

'Good heavens, no! But I'm afraid he does do a little poaching from time to time.'

'So is it because of the gun he's got stuffed down his trouser leg that he has the bottom of his trousers tied with string? The string is there to make sure that the gun doesn't fall out?'

'That's part of it. But if he has shot a rabbit, a hare or a pheasant he'll put the corpse down his trouser leg if his pockets are full.'

'But you couldn't get a pheasant into a pocket!'

'You could if you had Thumper's pockets. He has two of them inside his jacket and they're called poacher's pockets. You could easily get quite a large animal into one of them.'

'Oh. I see. Do you approve of poaching, doctor?'

I laughed. 'Thumper says that birds and animals all belong to God. His argument is that they can't be considered to belong to the person who owns the land they're living on.'

'You didn't answer my question.'

'Patsy and I are vegetarian. But Thumper is my friend.'

'A very good friend, I should think. He seems a very kind fellow.'

'He's a very good friend and a very kind fellow,' I agreed. 'You aren't the only villager he's helped. You could travel a long way on a fast horse without finding a kinder, more generous man.'

I told her that it was Thumper who, with my predecessor Dr Brownlow, had first made me welcome in Bilbury. It was Thumper who helped me find my first car.

'Do you think I should pay him something for helping me?' she asked.

'No,' I said. 'Definitely not.'

'But he doesn't look terribly well off. He looks very scruffy and that old truck of his has obviously seen better days.'

'He likes doing things for people,' I told her.

'Maybe I'll let him have some cherries when they're properly ripe – if the birds have left me some.'

'I'm sure he would be grateful. Or just let him pick up the fallen branches in your garden. He'll cut them up for you. And you've got a couple of fruit trees that are dead and need taking down. Apple, pear and cherry all make good firewood. You can then share the logs with Thumper.'

Mrs Peters agreed that this sounded an excellent idea and a perfectly equitable arrangement.

She made an excellent recovery and after that I called in to see her once or month or so. She had fewer ailments than most people half her age and apart from that initial illness she was never ill.

It was a couple of weeks after her 93rd birthday that Mrs Peters admitted to me that she had one regret.

'I have always been a careful woman,' she told me. 'When I was a young girl I was always frighteningly well-behaved. I suppose I didn't have much choice – since my father was a bishop. I could hardly go round throwing stones through greenhouses, could I? And then I married a vicar and I remained discreet and law abiding. I never drove above the speed limit, I was always polite to shop assistants, even when they were terribly annoying, and I don't think I ever once lost my temper in public. In the Post Office I was always the one customer who stood there quietly and uncomplaining, however long the queues were and however slowly the counter clerks seemed to be working.'

'I have always been a rather trusting person, rather naïve even,' she continued. 'When I was a girl my parents took me to the theatre. It was, I think, what they used to call a variety show. The star, I remember, was a comedian called Jimmy Wheeler. When he came onto the stage he began his act with the line: 'A funny thing happened to me on the way to the theatre'. I'd never heard the phrase before, and I didn't realise it was a fairly traditional way for a comic to introduce a joke. I assumed that he was telling the truth and I was terribly impressed. I wondered just how far from the theatre this strange thing had happened and, most of all, I was impressed that he had arrived at the theatre without any material but had relied on observing something comical as he walked to the stage door. It seemed to me to show tremendous calm and confidence. When I mentioned this to my parents they looked puzzled, and a little sad, as though they had produced a daughter who was, to put it politely, a little slow. I don't think I was slow – just rather unworldly.'

'I never yearned to travel the world, I never had a need for a life filled with great excitements,' she said. 'I had a lovely, loving husband and although I've never been rich, I've always had a nice home. I always had plenty of books to read and I've always enjoyed the programmes on the wireless. I've had a wonderful life. No complaints.'

'I rather think there is a 'but' or a 'regret' waiting around the corner!' I said, when she paused. There was a faraway look in her eyes.

'Oh, I always hated that word 'but',' said Mrs Peters. 'I hated it especially when it came after a compliment. 'I really like your dress, but...' 'Your hair looks nice but...' 'How lovely the room looks but...'.' She laughed.

'So, what's the 'but'?'

'It isn't so much a 'but' as a 'regret',' said Mrs Peters. Suddenly, she seemed shy, as though she were worried that I might think what she was about to say rather strange.

'And so what's the regret?' I asked, pushing her a little.

'You're going to laugh.'

'No I'm not.'

'It's a really silly thing – and probably quite impossible.'

'Tell me and then I'll help you if I can.'

'I always wanted to climb a tree.'

I looked at her, not sure that I'd heard properly.

'I always wanted to climb a tree,' she repeated, clearly aware that I was having difficulty believing what I was pretty sure that I'd heard.

'A tree?'

'A tree.'

'Any particular tree?'

'When I was nine or ten I used to watch the other children climbing a tree that was visible from our house. Well, technically our home was a palace. Bishops live in palaces as you know. But there was a wonderful old oak tree just inside our gates. Lots of children used to climb it, girls as well as boys. And from my bedroom window I used to watch them.'

'Is the tree still there?' I asked.

'Oh good heavens, I don't know. I don't have the faintest. The palace has probably been turned into offices or converted into flats and the tree is probably a nice table and a dozen chairs. It doesn't matter because I don't want to climb that particular tree.'

'So, which tree would you like to climb?'

She looked shy and even rather coy but didn't reply.

'Which one?'

This time she answered. 'That cherry tree outside my bedroom window.'

I thought about it. And then I walked to the window and looked out. The branches of the cherry tree looked as if they could be climbed but the first branches didn't leave the trunk until about four feet from the ground.

'What are you thinking?' she asked. But there was a twinkle in her eye and I think she knew what was on my mind.

'You'll need a little help to get off the ground,' I told her.

She looked at me and this time, for the 92-year-old widow of a clergyman, she was definitely looking coy.

'Oh, I'll certainly need a little help!' she agreed.

'When do you want to try it?'

'If it were done when 'tis done then 'twere well it were done quickly!' She raised both eyebrows and put her head to one side, as though asking for my approval.

'Macbeth.'

'Of course. Macbeth talking to himself. In act one, scene seven. Inside the castle.'

'You know your Macbeth.'

'I love Shakespeare. I've read all the plays several times.'

'Shall we make tomorrow afternoon tree climbing day?'

'Not today?'

'It's been raining and the tree will be slippery. Also you'll need some help. I want to ask Thumper to come and give me a hand.'

'Thumper Robinson?'

'There's only Thumper!'

'Yes, I suppose so. He won't laugh will he?'

'No. He won't laugh.'

I telephoned Thumper straight away and asked if he could meet me at Mrs Peter's house at three o'clock the following afternoon. He could.

And so, the following day there were four of us standing at the base of Mrs Peters' cherry tree. Mrs Peters was, on my advice, wearing a pair of good stout shoes, a pair of corduroy trousers, a thick shirt and a pair of her thickest gardening gloves. I was very conscious of the fact that elderly skin can easily tear and, once torn, can be slow to mend. I didn't want her to get a skin infection. Thumper and I had put Mrs Peters' kitchen stepladder at the base of the tree. The fourth person there was Patsy. I had asked her to come along to help.

'Isn't that cheating?' Mrs Peters asked, when she saw the stepladder.

'Not at all!' said Thumper. 'Climbers use all sorts of aids – ropes, crampons and ice axes. You need a small step ladder to give you a helping hand – or foot – into that nice fork of the tree.'

'OK. So what do I do?'

'You climb up the stepladder until you're standing on the top step. And then you put a foot onto the fork in the tree.'

'And then?'

'Then we'll see!'

With Thumper and I standing one each side of the ladder, Mrs Peters climbed up the steps and then, rather gingerly, stepped onto the fork in the tree.

'Oh this is fantastic!' she cried, clearly delighted. 'Can I go higher?'

'If you think you can?'

'Oh I do!' she said. And she stepped onto the next fork a foot or so higher up the tree.'

'Hold the tree tightly and smile!' I told her, as Thumper moved the stepladder away so that it wouldn't appear in the picture. I then took my camera out of my pocket and took some photos of Mrs Peters up the tree.

'Oh that's marvellous!' she said, at this unexpected bonus. 'Can I have copies to send to all my friends?'

'Have the picture put on your Christmas cards!' suggested Thumper.

'That's a wonderful idea!' agreed Mrs Peters.

I then put the stepladder back into position and Patsy went up a few rungs to help Mrs Peters climb down.

It took rather longer for her to get down than it had taken for her to get up into the tree. Patsy came down holding onto her. Thumper and I held the stepladder to make sure that it didn't wobble.

When we were back indoors we celebrated the adventure with a bottle of champagne and a chocolate cake bought especially for the occasion from Peter Marshall's excellent emporium.

'This was the most exciting thing I've done for a long time,' said Mrs Peters, posing for more photographs with a glass of champagne in one hand a large slice of cake in the other.

'You can tell your friends that you went up the tree to pick your cherries,' said Thumper. 'Make it sound as if you climb a tree every day.'

Mrs Peters laughed. 'Oh, could I do that?'

'Of course you could.'

'I feel so very naughty,' she said. And she giggled. 'I don't think I've ever giggled before.'

It seemed a bit of a pity that she had to wait until she was 92-years-old before she could have a giggle in her life. But I was pleased that I helped to make the day that gave her the giggle.

The True Story of How the Duck and Puddle Got Its Name

It was Sunday and Patsy had gone off early to help her mother make jam.

Making jam is something the two of them do every autumn. It's a real family tradition and it usually takes them a couple of days of work to convert our home-grown strawberries, gooseberries, plums, raspberries, apples and other fruits into jam. Patsy's sister Adrienne, now Mrs Fogg, usually goes along to help though I gather from Patsy that her main role is that of taster.

I had been left alone with Ben, our faithful and now elderly dog, our trio of cats, the sheep and Cedric the pig to sort out a few things around the house.

The two tasks on my list were: first to clear out a blocked drain and second to try to do something about the washing machine which had developed some sort of obstruction.

We'd noticed the blocked drain only when waste water started to form a large puddle outside the back door. And we'd noticed that the washing machine wasn't draining properly when a large puddle appeared in the room which an estate agent would probably describe as our 'utility room' but which we prefer to think of as 'that funny little room with a cobble stone floor and a door which is so full of woodworm that bits fall off it if you shut it too hard'.

Finding workmen to come in and do such seemingly trivial chores is never easy. Even the handymen who have advertisements which promise 'No Job Too Small', and who, if they ever answer their telephones, do so with great enthusiasm, mysteriously seem to find themselves fully booked when you explain that you don't want them to put on a new roof, install a new kitchen or build a two-car garage with granny flat and workshop attached.

I had first of all tried ringing a man who is known locally as Dirty Dick. He is a drain specialist who is reputed to have been cleaning out drains in North Devon since drains were first invented, though this may be something of an exaggeration. He never wears gloves or overalls and doesn't seem to spend a great deal of money on soap. His real name is Cyril Hornby-Smythe and, surprisingly perhaps, he has a degree in Ancient Languages from Cambridge University. He lives in a huge, tumble-down house in Barnstaple. His wife teaches domestic science at a local secondary modern school.

Sadly, Dirty Dick wasn't available. His wife told me that he was in hospital having a hernia repaired and wouldn't be available for cleaning out drains for at least a month.

I told her I didn't think we could wait that long, asked her to pass on my best wishes to her husband for a speedy and uneventful recovery and tried another couple of drain specialists.

One of them said he could probably manage to do something in six weeks and the other had an answering machine with a message saying he was on holiday in the Seychelles for two months. I made a mental note to consider a career in drain cleaning if I ever found myself struck off the medical register and unable to continue practising medicine.

So, rather than waste any more time making useless calls on the telephone, I decided to try to clear the drain myself.

I did have a set of old drain rods, which I had found in a barn a few months earlier. I had no idea how old they were but they seemed serviceable so I fitted the rods together, pulled the drain cover off the nearest inspection point and set to work.

I didn't have the faintest idea what I ought to be doing but it seemed to me that if I stuck the rod with the little brush fixed on the end into the drain, and then used the other rods to enable me to push it into the drain as far as it would go, I might have a chance of clearing the blockage and sorting out the problem.

I pushed and pulled and eventually a great bundle of roots came out of the drain with the brush. As I did so there was much gurgling and eventually, after sounds which alarmed me so much that I actually stood up and moved back a few paces, the contents of the pipe started to move. Moments later the blockage had obviously gone for the sewer pipe was empty. I hadn't felt so pleased with myself since I managed to pass O level Latin at the first attempt.

To my absolute delight I then discovered that the drain which was blocked was the one into which the washing machine emptied, and that it was the blockage in the drain which was preventing the machine from draining effectively.

I had solved both problems at once.

I was so pleased with myself that for a very brief moment I considered putting an advertisement in the local paper and advertising my services as a handyman. If a drains specialist could earn enough to have a two month holiday in the Seychelles maybe I could earn enough to buy a new rear tyre for my bicycle or, at the very least, arrange to have the existing one mended. (The rear tyre had a slow puncture in it which meant that I either had to pump it up every time I used the bicycle or else bump along uncomfortably on a flat tyre.)

I have to admit that clearing out a blocked drain, and seeing the backed up water drain away out of the washing machine, was strangely satisfying. It reminded me of the time I catheterised Mr Edgar Turner and emptied two and a half pints of stale, second hand beer from his bladder.

When I'd done my chores I had a bath, put on fresh clothes and wandered down the garden for a while.

It had been a long, hard and rather difficult week.

The most significant, and saddest event, had been the death of George Meddlecott who had died during the week in extraordinary circumstances.

George, had been in his mid-40s, and had worked as a shepherd.

There really aren't any specialist shepherds around these days but back in the 1970s there were quite a few men (all the shepherds I knew were male) who spent their lives looking after sheep.

On the Tuesday of that week, George had been found dead in a field just a mile and a half away from Bilbury Grange. He had been stabbed three times in the stomach, and when his body was found by two walkers, I was called. I was, therefore, the one who saw the body and confirmed both that it was George Meddlecott and that he was dead. I called the police because it seemed rather suspicious to say the least.

Within two hours there were two dozen policemen in the field, including a Chief Superintendent, and murder was pretty obviously their first diagnosis.

However, this view was rather weakened by the discovery that the knife was George's own and that the only fingerprints on it belonged to him.

On Thursday the police talked at length to George's brother and found that George had for weeks been suffering from pain caused by terrible wind.

George's brother lived in Barnstaple and worked in a bank. He said that George had steadfastly refused either to come and talk to me about it or to take any of the remedies his brother had offered in an attempt to find a solution. He had also refused point blank to amend his diet in any way. (I knew that George lived on a strange diet, which seemed to consist largely of food he had scavenged from fields, hedgerows and the waste bins outside the Duck and Puddle and Peter Marshall's shop. He spent most of the pittance he earned on pipe tobacco and bottled beer.)

On Friday, the police concluded that George hadn't been murdered but had accidentally killed himself. Because he was a shepherd he knew that a common, old remedy for sheep which were swollen with wind was to stab them in the stomach in order to release the accumulated gas. (If you don't release the gas the bloated sheep may fall over and be stranded on its back, vulnerable to birds who will peck out its eyes and then peck it to death.)

George had apparently mentioned this to his brother and had asked if he thought it might work on a human being. Amazingly, the brother had failed to mention this to anyone and had simply replied that he didn't know.

The conclusion was that poor George had tried to save himself from the pain by stabbing himself in order to release the awful wind he was experiencing. (The pain of trapped wind is widely and massively underestimated). He had then bled to death and died, alone and in the middle of a field.

Other than seeing the dead body, and confirming that George was dead, I hadn't really been involved since I had never seen him as a patient, but the police had been to visit me at least half a dozen times to ask for information. I found it difficult to imagine how desperate poor George must have been to take such drastic action.

And so, after successfully clearing both the drain and the washing machine blockage, I wandered down the garden in search of a little peace.

Ben, the three cats (Emily, Sophia and Jeremy) and the sheep (Lizzie, Petulia, Cynthia, Sarah-Louise and Miss Houdini) all followed me.

It was difficult to walk about in our garden without becoming part of a procession and I sometimes used to feel that I needed a stick to twirl or a big drum to beat.

It was fortunate, I suppose, that Cedric, the pig we had on loan from his American owners, was fast asleep in his sty, having just finished an enormous breakfast of his favourite fresh fruit and vegetable platter. I'm afraid that Cedric, like all the animals who lived with us, was rather spoilt. He used to enjoy going for a walk

I picked an apple off one of the late fruiting trees and tossed it to Percy, our tame pheasant. There were plenty of windfalls from the trees which had already produced their crop but Percy was a fussy bird. He ate a third of the apple and then wandered off. The minute he'd gone, a crow pierced the remains with his beak and flew off with it. Then a squirrel and two rabbits appeared on the lawn and sat there looking rather pathetic and starved.

Feeling rather as though I'd wandered into a Walt Disney movie, I plucked three more apples and threw them in their direction. Rabbits and squirrels love apples – or at least our rabbits and squirrels did. In the really bad weather I sometimes used to pop an apple down a rabbit hole so that the rabbits snuggling together down below have a little something extra to munch.

Then Percy returned, looking for his missing apple. So I gave him another. This time he ate just a third of it before wandering off for a drink of water. A seagull swooped and picked up the two thirds of an apple in his beak and flew away to enjoy a quiet feast somewhere else in the garden. It occurred to me that at the rate I was going I would soon have to explain to Patsy why we had such a poor apple crop. Another crow flew down and started to peck at a windfall apple. Then a seagull appeared and clearly wanted to take the apple away from him. (There were scores of other windfalls on the ground which the badgers hadn't yet eaten but the seagull wanted that apple and no other apple would do. Birds are just like small children.) I then watched in astonishment as a bunch of other crows flew down and stood around their chum so that he could eat his apple in peace. That was truly altruistic behaviour for the guard crows got nothing out of the exercise except the knowledge that they were looking after their pal.

I watched all this happening in awe and I truly felt lucky to be living in such a wonderful home in such a marvellous part of the world. North Devon is the coldest part of the county, raw with wind and rain in the winter, but there is a wildness about it which seems to produce a sense of family among the residents – both human and otherwise.

In my early years in Bilbury, when Dr Brownlow, my predecessor, had still been alive, I had travelled a fair amount – mainly to London or to towns and cities where there were television studios or radio stations. On several occasions Patsy and I had gone to London together. Our greatest joy had been merely walking through the streets of London, looking in shop windows and being astonished by the speed at which life was lived. Our favourite walk was to start at Trafalgar Square, walk up Charing Cross Road (calling in at one or two of the second hand bookshops en route), then turn left at Cambridge Circus and go along Shaftsbury Avenue to Piccadilly Circus. When we got to Piccadilly Circus we would walk along Piccadilly, turning right into the Burlington Arcade and then up Bond Street. We usually then took a taxi back to Paddington Station rather than struggle along Oxford Street. We liked this walk best at dusk on a slightly drizzly autumn evening, and we did it many times. I don't know why we liked that route or why we liked walking it when it was drizzly and going dark. I suppose it just seemed more romantic. Sometimes we would stop off for afternoon tea at Fortnum and Mason where a pot of tea for two and a couple of toasted tea cakes would cost us a small fortune but make us feel rich for a few moments.

During those years I had made a considerable number of television programmes (most of which had been of the instantly forgettable kind) and had spent rather too much time promoting my books by doing interviews with young presenters who didn't have the faintest idea who I was, hadn't bothered to look at the book I was promoting (let alone actually read it) and who clearly cared more about whether their make-up was perfect, their hair just so and their smile was offering just the right mixture of charm, humour and integrity than they did about the subject we were supposed to be discussing.

But within a year or two my travels outside Bilbury had been strictly limited by my solo responsibilities for the health of the village.

After the death of Dr Brownlow, it was no longer really possible for me to leave the village – for the very simple reason that there was no one else to take my surgeries, do my visits or answer my emergency calls. I could, and occasionally did, pop into Barnstaple, Combe Martin, South Molton, Ilfracombe or Lynton but expeditions further afield were impossible. Even Exeter, the county town of Devon, had become a foreign country to me. There was a relatively brief period when my practice was shut down by the NHS because it was considered inefficient to have a solitary doctor providing medical care for a relatively small village. For a while I earned my living solely from my writing. But after protests from the villagers, things soon went back to normal and I was soon working as a GP again. And there were no more trips to London or, indeed, to anywhere else. The village of Bilbury was so spread out and confusing that it would have been impossible to find a locum doctor who could find Myrtle Cottage at three o'clock in the morning on a rainy night. And if we'd gone away from Bilbury Grange, who on earth would have looked after our menagerie?

And the truth was that I really didn't mind at all that I had to stay in Bilbury.

By the time I stopped going there, London had seemed to me to have become dirty, over-crowded and just too busy.

The last time I'd been there, I had found it difficult to believe that on the 6th of October, 1897, the author Arnold Bennett had walked through Green Park, just yards from Buckingham Palace, and, looking through an October mist, had seen sheep grazing in the park. By the early 1970s, a visit to London left me coughing and wheezing (and with a grime-encrusted shirt).

I'm happy to accept that my attitude to London said far more about me than it did about London. It is perfectly possible that London was no different to the way it had always been and that it was me, not England's capital city, who had changed. I had fallen in love with country living and I felt that I would be quite happy if I never again had to board an aeroplane, climb onto a train or struggle through a bustling crowd of commuters and shoppers.

Meanwhile, I stood in the garden and looked around.

Our resident pheasant, the one whom we had Christened Lord Percival (but knew as Percy – he didn't seem to mind this familiarity), was now standing beside our summerhouse flapping his wings and calling loudly. He did this for a few minutes and then wandered off up the garden to the spot among some rhododendron bushes where he roosts. Ten minutes later a hen pheasant appeared, clearly attracted by Lord Percival's attractive courting calls. Unfortunately, Lord Percival was now nowhere to be seen. The hen waited a while, wandered around on the lawn and then, looking sad, doubtless disappointed and frustrated, she wandered off again.

I watched three rabbits munching away at the grass and thought how good it was of them to help keep the lawn under control. Rabbits make excellent lawn mowers. I reckoned that I had to cut the grass only half as often as I would have had to cut it without them. And for the first time I saw a rabbit doing what is called a binky. When a rabbit suddenly jumps into the air and twists about before landing, it is doing a binky. When a lamb or a sheep does it this is called pronging.

It is said in books that squirrels never drink water but this is not true. We have several squirrels who regularly drink from our bird bath. The wild creatures use the bird bath for all sorts of things in addition to drinking and washing. I once saw one of the squirrels who lived with us take a hazelnut which had fallen in some mud over to the bird bath and give it a good wash before eating it. I've also watched a robin pull a worm out of the grass, take it to the bird bath and wash it and then gave it to another robin perched in a tree nearby.

Those who study animal behaviour insist that we must never anthropomorphise. But I find it difficult not to and I am quietly convinced that animals have far more complicated lives than some would imagine. It has for years been assumed that only human beings are capable of thought processes. I believe that this is hubristic nonsense. My own studies of animals have convinced me that they are capable of very complex behavioural patterns which could not exist without complex thought processes.

I don't think I am alone in this. Thousands of individuals who have shared their lives with dogs and cats, for example, will confirm that animals are not the simple mechanical creatures that Descartes would have us believe them to be. And why on earth should they be? After all, primates such as orang-utans share 97% of our own DNA. They can communicate with one another and they show skills with tools – as well as having a sense of humour. Elephants and chimpanzees display compassion, treat themselves with medicines when they are ill and mourn their friends and relations. And there is plenty of evidence that animals can love.

Birds too are capable of extraordinary thought processes. All members of the corvid family (which includes ravens, crows, rooks, magpies, jays and jackdaws) have much more complex brains than most people imagine and many studies have shown the wisdom of these creatures. Ravens and rooks, for example, have been shown to maintain long-term relationships with other birds, and their social and political systems are often as complex as our own.

I wandered around the garden for the best part of an hour, just looking and watching and learning.

When I first came to live in Bilbury I would walk through the lanes quite quickly, more intent on where I was going than on where I was. And I now knew that most of the visitors, hikers and walkers, who wandered through the village did so at such a pace that they actually saw very little of the world around them. To see and understand the countryside, and the creatures in it, you have to be prepared to stand and lean on a five barred gate occasionally; and to be prepared to look and to listen. And there are so many fascinating things to see. I had learnt so much in my years at Bilbury Grange. I'd learned that ants move around far more speedily when the weather is warm. You would think it would be the other way round and that they would run around when it was cold. But they don't. They speed up when it's warm. I found myself fascinated by the woodlouse too. You can find woodlice in crumbling old logs and, when the weather is bad, they come indoors. The woodlouse used to be called the 'pill woodlouse' because if threatened they roll themselves up into a ball. Doctors used to prescribe them for a variety of ailments. Can you imagine being told by your doctor: 'Go home and take two woodlice every four hours. Send a boy with a message in the morning if there is no improvement'.

As soon as the sun told me that it was approaching noon I wandered back up to the house, climbed onto my rather rusty old bicycle (after pumping up the back tyre) and pedalled slowly along the lanes to the Duck and Puddle where I had arranged to meet Thumper and Patchy for a little light luncheon. Ben wandered along behind me. She knew exactly where we were heading and, like most of the inhabitants of our village, was content to get there at her own pace.

When I arrived at the pub I found my two pals already there, settled beside the usual log fire and already topping up their blood alcohol levels. They had not yet started to do anything to contribute to their blood cholesterol levels. Frank, who was sitting with them, was sipping a glass of bubbly tonic water. Harry, the more than slightly over-qualified new barman, was standing behind the bar polishing glasses with a tea towel. Whenever I saw him there, I wondered if there were any other barmen in North Devon with a medical degree. I wondered how many of the men and women polishing glasses and pulling pints had once held an eminent position at a London teaching hospital.

To my surprise there were two other customers in the Duck and Puddle. He was short and thin with very short hair. She was shorter and thinner and also had very short hair. They were clearly motorists rather than walkers or cyclists. I knew this from their smart, clean clothing, their neatly combed hair, their un-flushed faces and the fact that there was a smart, little motor car that I'd never seen before parked outside in the Duck and Puddle car park. I hadn't noticed what make it was. When I was a boy I used to be able to identify most of the cars on the road but by the early 1970s I found that most cars looked much the same as one another and unless I was looking at something exotic, exceptionally expensive or vintage, I wasn't able to tell one from the other.

'Stanley and Stiffy Sidwell,' said the male stranger, introducing both himself and a woman whom I assumed was his wife as I entered. He had that way of speaking that I had only before heard from the mouths of former diplomats. Maybe it's a style that is also taught to health and safety specialists for that is what he turned out to be. It's an odd way of speaking: strangely formal, flat, superior and condescending. I suppose it's taught as a way of talking down to the natives; calming them when trying to persuade them to put down their spears and abandon the idea to pop you into the hot pot. I didn't know why he introduced his wife as well as himself, though it did occur to me, quite wrongly, that maybe she couldn't speak, or had a

48

sore throat. Still, she didn't seem to mind this modest act of lese-majeste so I didn't see why I should mind. At first glance, I thought he looked rather miserable; along the lines of a man who has just discovered that while he was having a nap some miscreant had snuck in and nicked his liver and mischievously replaced it with one of those little models of a lighthouse filled with layers of different coloured sand.

He was drinking what looked like coffee and she was drinking something that was probably tea. The Duck and Puddle specialises in alcoholic beverages and filling food and does not pretend to be a coffee house. If it ever appeared in one of those guide books which provide marks and criticisms, the Duck and Puddle would not receive anything more than two stars for its hot beverages and even then one of the stars would doubtless be for the fact that when someone asks for a warm cup of something they are invariably served something that is unquestionably hot. 'We might not make the best cup of coffee in the world,' Frank had once told a customer, 'but we make the hottest.'

I told Stanley my name, took his outstretched hand and shook it. He had a small, toothbrush sized moustache, only slightly bigger than the one favoured by A. Hitler Esq and one of those limp, slightly moist handshakes that always make me want to wipe my hand down the side of my trousers afterwards. I managed to resist the temptation to do this. Stiffy also held out her hand and hers, too, was one of those insipid handshakes that makes you wonder if it has actually taken place at all. He told me that I should call him Stanley and that his wife answered to Stiffy.

'I'm a Health and Safety Inspector,' said Stanley. 'But we're on holiday at the moment. We're on a tour of English inns and taverns. This is our third inn of the day.'

I was clearly expected to be impressed by this and, not wanting to be churlish or unwelcoming, I did my best to look impressed. At the same time Ben pushed open the front door, wandered over to the rug by the fire and lay down. She used to race around Bilbury. But she had become much more stately and measured. Frank immediately stood up and fetched her a bag of her favourite pork scratchings.

'I thought you'd like to try this, for a change,' said Harry, handing me a tumbler containing Laphroaig whisky. 'I'm sure you'll prefer it to your usual brand of lemonade.'

49

Stanley looked across at me, nodded and smiled. He and Stiffy had remained standing at the bar, rather than sitting down and making themselves comfortable. The pair of them looked as though there were a pair of lecturers about to start giving a lecture. Little did I know how accurate this appraisal was going to prove to be.

'Dandelion and Burdock,' Harry explained to Stanley. 'It's made locally according to a 17th century recipe.'

I hoped that Stanley didn't have a particularly well-trained sense of smell. Laphroaig malt whisky doesn't smell much like Dandelion and Burdock.

'You shouldn't give those to a dog,' said Stiffy pointing at Ben and the pork scratchings. 'I'm a supervisor.' She didn't say what she supervised and none of us liked to ask.

Frank looked at her and then at me.

'They contain too much fat for dogs,' the woman explained. 'And I've read that they can cause problems in the dog's pancreas.'

'They contain too much fat for people,' said Thumper.

'She only has them occasionally,' I said, feeling rather guilty. I looked across at Ben to see if it was too late to take the pork scratchings away from her. It wasn't too late but I couldn't bear to do it. Like all of us she likes an occasional treat – even if it is bad for her. I wondered if I should mention to Stanley and Stiffy that the caffeine in tea and coffee can cause cancer of the pancreas. I decided not to bother.

'My husband is an expert on inn signs and names,' said Stiffy. 'We're writing a book about them.'

'Stiffy takes the photographs,' added Stanley.

And for the first time I noticed that Stiffy had a camera slung round her neck. It was something fancy with lots of levers and dials and a complicated looking lens. 'I hope you won't mind my mentioning it,' he said, talking to Harry and moving the fireside rug with the toe of his shoe. 'But this rug is loose. Rugs in establishments where the public are allowed access are required to be fastened down to avoid accidents.'

'Ah,' said Harry, without hesitation. 'I wish we could do that. We've been asking them for years to let us fix it down. Unfortunately, the rug has been designated a floor covering of outstanding natural beauty and of significant historical interest by the Government's Ancient Rugs and Artefacts Department. They won't let us move it, nail it down or even put any sticky stuff on the back.'

'Not allowed to impede its movement in any way, was the phrase I think you mentioned,' said Patchy who had, for some reason known only to himself decided to deliver this in a rather broad country yokel accent. Patchy is one of the best educated and best read men I knew. He had what used to be called a cut-glass accent.

'It's not been moved for years,' said Frank. 'It's been here longer than I have. I wouldn't dare move it for fear of what we might find underneath it.'

'Blood stains, probably,' added Thumper. 'From that murder.'
We all looked at him.

'Sorry,' Thumper said. 'I know no one likes to talk about that.'

'Don't worry about it,' muttered Frank. 'I know I'll have to talk about it one day.'

'It really wasn't your fault,' said Thumper.

'Everyone agrees they both asked for it,' said Patchy. 'I don't know what they were thinking of – behaving like that in front of your very eyes.'

There was a long silence. We all sipped our drinks. Ben continued crunching her pork scratchings.

It was Stiffy who eventually spoke.

'Yours is a very interesting establishment,' she said. She looked around as she spoke. She clearly wasn't quite sure who she should be addressing. 'Are your beams real?'

Frank frowned and looked at her sternly. Asking him if his beams were real was about as tactless as asking a bathukolpian woman you've just met if her breasts were real. 'Real?' he said. He managed to stretch the word out until the elastic seemed certain to break. He reminded me of Dame Edith Evans playing Lady Bracknell in Oscar Wilde's 'The Importance of Being Earnest' – the famous bit where she is shocked about John Worthington's provenance and she says: 'A handbag?'

'Or are they just glued on?' continued Stiffy. 'A lot of public houses have their beams glued on. We saw one in Exeter which had polystyrene beams.' Stiffy did not seem aware that her initial query had upset the landlord and that her supplementary remarks were just making things worse.

51

Frank glared at her. 'The Duck and Puddle is a very old and original pub. The only stuff in here that's false is in my mouth and they're called dentures!' he said. Frank was rightly proud of what he and Gilly had built. I could understand why he was feeling aggrieved.

'They sometimes do it to make the place look old,' explained Stanley, unthinkingly making things worse.

'My husband is something of an expert on many aspects of public house presentation,' said Stiffy who, it seemed to me, could probably win prizes for insensitivity, indifference and an inability to tell when someone was upset. 'The publishers expect my husband's tome on inn signs to be a seminal work. And it is bound to be an international bestseller.'

'Seminal,' said Patchy, nodding. He said it again and looked at Thumper who also nodded.

'You can trace public house names back to the Crusades,' said Stanley. 'The people commemorated the crusades with names such as 'The Saracen's Head' and 'The Trip to Jerusalem'. There are still public houses in Britain with such names.'

'Some public houses are named after the occupation of the proprietor,' said Stiffy. 'So drinking houses were called 'The Wheatsheaf' if the owner was a baker, 'The Horseshoe' or 'The Three Horseshoes' if he was a farrier and 'The Three Compasses' if he was a carpenter.'

"The Green Man' denoted that the pub was kept by a game keeper, 'The Woodman' that the publican was a forester and 'The Coach and Horses' made it clear that the pub was originally run by a coachman,' said Stanley. "The Blacksmith's Arms' and 'The Cobbler's Arms' are pretty explanatory.'

I got the impression this wasn't the first time that Stanley and Stiffy had recited these names. They seemed to have worked up a little double act. The Stanley and Stiffy Show. 'Of course some pubs were named for other reasons, so a pub called 'Bag o'Nails' would be named after the ancient Greek ceremony celebrating the bacchanals,' said Stanley.

'The seven most popular pub names are all expressions of support for royalty,' said Stiffy. 'Stanley has determined that there are over 600 pubs in the United Kingdom called 'The Red Lion' because that was the badge favoured by James the First. He made it a law that premises selling alcohol should all stick up pictures or models of a lion. He insisted that when he travelled from Edinburgh to London he wanted to see lions everywhere he went.'

'There are scores of pubs called 'The Crown', 'The Rose and Crown', 'The Crown and Anchor', 'The King's Head' and 'The Queen's Head',' Stanley informed us. 'Pubs called 'The Royal Oak' are so named because Charles II hid in an oak tree in 1651 after the disastrous battle of Worcester.'

'Some pubs were called 'The White Hart' because that was the badge of Richard II, and some were called the So and So Arms after the name of a local bigwig. And then there are public houses which were named directly after the coat of arms of a local dignitary. So many inns and taverns in Warwickshire were called the 'Bear and Staff' because that was the coat of arms of the Earl of Warwick.'

Looking around I could see that I wasn't alone in thinking that we'd pretty well reached our limit on this particular subject. But Stanley and Stiffy weren't finished yet. They told us that some pub names were either simply fantastic or comical, and based on old wives' tales and local legends. So, said Stanley, there are pubs called 'World Turned Upside Down', 'Cat and Mutton', 'Castle of Comfort', 'Merry Month of May', 'Labour in Vain', 'Tippling Philosopher', 'Darby and Joan', 'Baker and Basket', 'Magnet and Dewdrop', 'The Old Friends', 'Mrs Grundy's Arms' and 'Who'd Have Thought It?'.

'Of course some pubs get nicknames,' said Stiffy. "The White Swan in Stratford-upon-Avon, next to the Shakespeare theatre, is known to everyone as The Dirty Duck and is regularly patronised by actors, fans and hangers on.'

'My own particular interest is the pub sign,' said Stanley. 'In mediaeval days there was no bigger advertising space than the local pub sign and inn keepers spent a good deal of money on their signs. 'The White Hart' at Scole in Norfolk had a famous sign which stretched right across the road and consisted of 25 life-size, classical and mythological figures. The sign cost over £1,000 which was a lot of money in the 17th century. Many other pub signs were painted by famous artists. So, for example, Hogarth did a sign for a pub called 'The Man Loaded with Mischief'. Some old pub signs are now so valuable they've been taken down and are displayed under glass or have been sold to collectors and museums.'

'Tell the nice people about how the Duck and Puddle got its name,' said Stiffy, addressing her husband.

I glanced around and could see that none of my chums seemed particularly happy at being described as 'nice people'. It seemed to me to be almost as insulting as being described as 'little people'.

Before her husband could say anything, Stiffy turned back to address us. 'Before we came in Stanley did a little research work, using the reference books he carries in the car, and explained to me where this public house got its name.'

'Oh, I doubt if these good people would really want to hear my opinion,' said Stanley.

'Oh but we would!' insisted Harry immediately.

'Absolutely!' agreed Patchy.

The rest of us muttered our slightly muted encouragement. Only Ben, who had now finished her pork scratchings, remained silent. I know that my encouragement was entirely fake. To be perfectly honest I just wanted Stanley and Stiffy to finish their double act, climb back into their little car and chug off to the next stop on their itinerary. I knew from the way they spoke that Thumper, Patchy, Frank and Harry all felt as I did.

'Well, it's just my supposition, of course,' said Stanley, with unexpected modesty. 'One can never be entirely certain about these things, particularly where history is involved. But I would think that the word 'duck' is merely a bastardisation of the word 'Duke', and the word 'puddle' is probably taken from the verb 'to puddle' which was used to describe the manufacturing process which enabled an iron foundry to turn molten iron into malleable iron. Do any of you know if there was ever an iron foundry in the area?' He looked around enquiringly.

'There's never been anything like that round here,' said Thumper who was born and brought up in Bilbury. There is no doubt that if there had ever been an iron foundry in the area he would have known about it.

'Well, if there really wasn't a foundry,' said Stanley, making it clear he didn't accept Thumper's assurance that there hadn't been, 'then there should have been one. Maybe there were plans for one but the foundry never materialised.'

No one said anything.

Stiffy picked up her cup, emptied it and put it back down on the bar counter.

'Of course, the Duke concerned was probably not the Duke of Devonshire, whose seat is, of course, Chatsworth House in Derbyshire, but the Earl of Devon,' continued Stanley with a doggedness you had to admire. 'The first Earl of Devon was Baldwin de Redvers, whose seat was Carisbroke Castle. He was driven out of England to France where he joined the Empress Matilda. And it was the Empress Matilda who gave Redvers the title Earl of Devon. Locally, among the citizens, it is quite likely that he would have been known as the Duke though we do also know that a man called James Askew-Herrington, who lived in Devon in the 19th century, was known to describe himself as the Duke of Devon and so we must bear him in mind as a possibility.'

'So, you think the pub got its name from a Duke and an iron foundry?' said Frank.

'I think that is the most likely possibility,' said Stanley with a sage nod. 'I think we can ignore the possibility that the word 'puddle' is a bastardisation of the word 'paddle', which was the common name for a lump fish in the 16th century. But there is one other possibility which I can't entirely rule out.'

'And what's that?' asked Frank.

I think it is fair to say that I could tell that he didn't seem entirely convinced by Stanley's analysis of how the pub had acquired its unusual name.

'Well, although it isn't entirely well-known, poodles were at one time regarded as excellent hunting dogs – particularly where there was water nearby. They had quick reflexes, were renowned for being able to spot where a bird had fallen and were widely used by huntsmen as early as the 17th century. So it's easy to see that the pub's name could describe the type of bird that was commonly hunted in the area and the type of dog used to collect the bird.'

Stanley leant back, folded his arms and assumed a classic 'What do you think of that, then?' pose.

We all looked at Frank. Frank looked at the floor.

'Marvellous!' said Harry Stottle with enormous enthusiasm. Actually, he didn't so much say it as boom it. 'That was quite exceptional; the apotheosis of obscurantism! You cut through the embranglements of history with exoptable and magniloquent obnubilation!'

Stanley, frowned, as though trying to decide whether this was, or was not, a compliment. . 'Thank you!' he said eventually, clearly preferring to assume that the barman had congratulated him. It was, perhaps, not the language he had expected to hear coming from the other side of the bar in a country pub. He was not to know the concatenation of circumstances which had led the former Dr Pelham Ronald Eckersley, a psychiatrist, to abandon his private Harley Street consulting practice, and a teaching post at what he himself called a 'snotty' London teaching hospital, and to run away to the West Country, to Devon, to Bilbury and finally to the Duck and Puddle.

'It's so nice to find people who are able to understand and appreciate Stanley's work,' said Stiffy.

'It's very kind of you, I'm sure,' said Stanley. He smiled and lowered his eyes modestly. I thought he looked like a young, teenage girl who has been told that her hair looks nice or that the dress she is wearing is very pretty. Well, as much as a Health and Safety Inspector with a toothbrush moustache can look like a teenage girl.

Suddenly, Stanley looked at his watch. 'Is that really the time? We ought to be getting on.'

'We have a time table, you see,' said Stiffy. She took a piece of card out of her pocket and examined it. She then put the card back into her pocket and checked her watch. 'We were due to be at 'The Pack of Cards' in Combe Martin ten minutes ago,' she said to her husband.

'Good heavens!' said Stanley. 'Time flies when you're enjoying good conversation with good company, doesn't it?'

We all murmured, the way people do when they want to seem to agree with something but don't want to come right out and agree with it with real words.

And so Stanley and Stiffy left and a moment later we heard their little car chug away from The Duck and Puddle, from Bilbury and, quite probably, out of our lives for ever.

'They've gone the wrong way,' said Patchy, who had stood up to watch them go. 'They're taken the lane down to Softly's Bottom. If they're lucky they'll end up in Lynmouth. If they're unlucky no one will ever see them again.'

'Lucky for 'The Pack of Cards',' said Thumper.

'What was that you said to Stanley?' Frank asked Harry. 'That apotheosis stuff?'

'Oh, I just congratulated him on his spirited balderdash,' replied the barman. 'It was a load of old bollocks wasn't it Frank?'

Frank nodded.

'I asked how the pub got its name two months ago,' admitted Harry. 'So I knew that our Stanley was talking gibberish. But he was enjoying himself so much that it seemed a pity to tell him the truth.'

'So, how did the Duck and Puddle get its name?' I asked.

It occurred to me, with some shame and not a little embarrassment, that I'd never asked this before. I could tell by the way Thumper and Patchy leant forward with interest that they also didn't know how the pub had acquired its unusual name.

'Our pub used to be called 'The White Hart',' said Frank. 'When Gilly and I bought the pub, half a lifetime ago, it was run down and in an even worse state than it is now. The sign had fallen into the road and, the pub had no customers. When we took over we discovered that there are hundreds of pubs in Devon called 'The White Hart' so we wanted to start afresh, call it something different.'

'So where did the name come from?' I asked.

'When we got here it was winter and it had been raining and there was a huge puddle in the space that is now the car park.'

We all groaned.

'Is this true?' asked Patchy.

'Honest, it's true,' said Frank. Harry, who had heard the story already, nodded his agreement. 'You can ask Gilly. She'll tell you the same.'

'And there was just the one duck on the pond?'

'A mallard,' said Frank. 'A duck. Nice girl. I don't know what happened to her. I like to think she just buggered off one day; that maybe a handsome drake flew in and they went off together to find a bigger puddle somewhere and fill it with ducklings. When they'd gone we had the hole filled in and now it's the car park.'

'Just one duck on a pond,' said Thumper reflectively. He frowned. 'You know, I grew up with this pub being the Duck and

Puddle. I don't remember it as anything else. And I always thought there was some wonderfully complicated reason for the name.'

'It's a pity you didn't tell Stanley the truth,' said Patchy. 'I'd loved to have seen his face.'

'Oh no,' I said. 'It was much better to let him go away and put his theory into his book.'

Patchy thought about it and laughed. 'You're right! It was much better that way.'

'I think it's a pretty wonderful way to name a pub,' said Harry.

And, without having to think any more about it, we all agreed with him.

'I'm glad Stanley and Stiffy have gone,' said Thumper. 'There was a horrid smell in here.'

'Yes, I could smell something funny,' agreed Patchy. 'I thought it was Stanley and Stiffy though I didn't really notice it until they'd been here a while. I thought perhaps they'd trodden in something or maybe eaten too many Brussels sprouts.'

Everyone sniffed, in the way that people do when they think there's a funny smell in the air.

'The smell hasn't gone,' said Harry. He looked at his watch, lifted the bar flap and came out from behind the bar. 'I've got to get a move on,' I said. 'Mildred's got a gig in Combe Martin and I've promised to drive her down there. She's in a bit of state now that she's lost her licence. Besides, I promised to be there to cheer her on.'

Mildred Snodgrass (whose stage name is 'Melina Melons') is a friend of a local stripper called Carole Singer, and like Mrs Singer she earns a living taking off her clothes in public houses.

Gengolphus (or Harry) and Mildred (or Maisie on Tuesday, Thursday and Sunday afternoons and Monday, Wednesday, Friday and Saturday evenings) were, as people used to say, 'going steady' and they certainly seemed extremely fond of each other.

I knew that Harry Stottle had not yet confessed to Mildred that his real name was Dr Eckersley and that in a previous existence he had been an eminent psychiatrist with a flourishing celebrity practice in Harley Street. Harry, who appeared to have mellowed enormously after finding love, had admitted to me that he was worried that Mildred might be disappointed, or even critical, when she found out that he hadn't always been a barman. 'She likes me being a barman,' he said. 'She seems to think it's a good, solid, respectable job for a fellow. She says you know where you are with a barman.'

Since I happened to know that Mrs Snodgrass had previously been married to a man who stole cars for a living I was not as surprised by this as some folk might have been. When you've spent a few years living with a man who carries a bent coat hanger in his jacket pocket and has an impressive collection of spare car number plates hidden in the garage, then any man with a job which involves working hours and a weekly wage packet must seem to be an enviably respectable alternative. Still, I didn't think she would object too much when she found that Harry hadn't always pumped pints for a living.

'Crumbs, do you need a licence to do that now?' I asked.

'Do what?'

'To take off your clothes in public?'

'Why would you need a licence to do that?'

'I've no idea. You seem to need a licence for just about everything these days. You have to have a licence to take a pig for a walk so it doesn't seem entirely unreasonable that you'd need a licence to take your clothes off in a pub. I suppose the authorities might think that if you didn't have to have a licence then everyone would be doing it.'

'No, you idiot!' said Harry. 'Mildred has lost her driving licence. She tried driving home after two glasses of port and lemon and did her best to flatten a lamp post.'

'It still smells a bit like drains in here,' said Thumper. He turned to Frank. 'I thought it was that pair of walkers, but they've gone now. Have you got a blockage somewhere down below?'

Frank frowned, thought for a moment and then shook his head. 'Not that I know of.'

Tentatively, I sniffed. I too could smell drains. And even after a bath and a change of clothes, I knew where the smell was coming from. I looked at my watch.

'Gosh, is that the time! I must fly. I've got a pile of paperwork to get through.'

And I hurried home to have another bath before Patsy got back from the preserve-making jamboree.

Blanche Manders

Mrs Blanche Manders came into my surgery, sat down, looked at me for a moment and burst into tears. She didn't just cry; she sobbed.

Mrs Manders lived on the outskirts of Bilbury, on the road leading out towards Barnstaple, and although I knew her by sight and by name, I knew I'd only rarely seen her as a patient. She had been taking the contraceptive pill since her marriage five years earlier but that was the only thing for which I had seen her. The only other entry on her cardboard medical file was in Dr Brownlow's handwriting and dated nine years earlier – before I'd first moved to Bilbury. She'd been to the surgery complaining of a sore throat. Dr Brownlow had prescribed an antibiotic. She hadn't returned so it seemed fair to assume that the antibiotic had worked and the sore throat had gone. She had been in her early twenties then and she was now just 29-years-old.

I pushed the box of paper tissues across the desk towards her and then moved my chair so that we were a little closer. I waited for the sobbing to subside before I said anything. At first the tears were pouring down her cheeks but slowly the crying slowed, as though she'd run out of tears. And then the sobbing was dry; her whole body wracked with the pain of whatever it was that was tormenting her. I coughed a little because the perfume she was wearing tickled my throat. She seemed to be wearing an awful lot of perfume for a trip to the doctor's surgery.

'What is it?' I asked. I spoke softly. She looked as if she had been crying all night; as though she hadn't slept a wink.

She tried to speak but she couldn't get any words out because when she tried, the sobbing got worse. It was dry now, no tears, but her whole body was wracked with every sob. I wondered what on earth it was that was causing her so much pain. I thought about what I knew of her family. According to her medical records, her parents were both dead and she had no brothers or sisters. There were, I was sure, no children. Just a husband called Harry. He was a few years older than her and worked for the council in Barnstaple. He was something in the planning department. As far as I could remember he was fighting fit. He was, I remembered, a keen cross country runner and like all long distance runners he was small, slightly built and thin.

'Has something happened to Harry?'

She shook her head.

'You have to tell me what it is.'

Still, she didn't speak.

'Have you been in pain? Have you found a lump? Are you bleeding?'

I thought that if I just asked her questions I might eventually trigger a response.

There was silence; a very loud, painful silence.

I asked more questions, searching for a key that would unlock the secret that was causing her so much pain.

'It's awful,' she whispered suddenly. 'I'm so ashamed.' She took a paper tissue from the box and blew her nose. Then she took another tissue and dried her eyes. Her eye make-up was smeared all over her cheeks by the crying. Wiping her eyes just made it worse.

'Talk to me,' I said.

'They say I smell.'

It was whispered so quietly that I wasn't sure I had heard properly. I asked her to repeat it.

'They say I smell.'

'Who says you smell?'

'The people I work with.'

Very tentatively, desperate not to make it obvious, I sniffed.

All I could smell was her perfume. I didn't know what brand it was but it was potent stuff. And she seemed to have used a lot of it.

And suddenly the floodgates opened. This time releasing words not tears. There was some pain, some anger, some frustration and some resentment.

'I bathe every day. I wash my hair twice a week. I go to the dentist regularly. I put on fresh clothes every day. What is wrong with me? What else can I do? I have never felt so ashamed in my life. Never!' She looked at me for the first time. 'What's wrong with me, doctor? Is there something wrong? You have to help me. You have to do something.'

61

'Who said that you smell? When did they say it?'

'Yesterday. My boss. I work in a clothes shop in Barnstaple and just before closing time he asked me to go into the office. I knew it was something bad because he wasn't his usual jolly self. He's normally very chatty and a bit flirty. He's the only man in the shop. Five women and him and he rather enjoys it, I think. I thought he was going to fire me and now I wish that was all it had been because I could have taken that. And anyway he might just as well have fired me because I can't ever go back there again.'

It took me another ten minutes to get the full story out of her.

It appeared that her boss had called her into his office, told her to sit down and then closed the door. He had then, rather bluntly and with absolutely no finesse, sympathy, understanding or care, told her that the other women in the shop had asked him to have a word with her because they said that she smelt. The boss, the shop manager, said that the other assistants had complained that they found her smell to be unpleasant and that they'd seen customers walk out of the shop when they'd smelt her.

And so then I understood the tears and the sobbing.

Many people would, I suspect, rather be told that they were stupid, or even accused of dishonesty, than be told that they smelt badly. To be told that you smell strikes at the very core of your being as a person; it is your very essence. To be told that you smell because you've trodden in something unpleasant is one thing, an irrelevance, but to be told that your body smells is a blow at your person. And for a woman it is, I suspect, even worse than it would be for a man. A man can laugh off such accusations and might even put it down to manliness – in the same way that a certain type of man might burp or fart in front of his workmates and laugh about it. He would probably be amused by a critical response. He would be unlikely to be broken in the way that Mrs Manders was broken.

'Did they say what the smell was like?' I asked her. 'All I can smell at the moment is your perfume.'

'Fish,' she said. 'They said I smelt of fish.'

She paused, took another tissue and blew her nose again. She put the used tissue into her handbag with the others. 'I used nearly a whole bottle of perfume before I came to see you.'

There are all sorts of disorders which can cause unusual or strong body smells. And as soon as Mrs Manders had told me her problem I started to go through them in my mind.

If a patient has diabetes then high levels of blood glucose can increase the incidence of bad breath and body odour. If diabetes gets out of control then a condition called diabetic ketoacidosis can develop. The body isn't getting enough insulin and so there is a shortage of the sugar the body needs for energy. One well-known sign of ketoacidosis is breath that smells rather fruity. It is a fairly easily identified smell.

But I didn't think that Mrs Manders had diabetes and if she had then I was sure it wasn't out of control. Besides, she had been told that she smelt of fish. Still, I could easily do a urine test that would tell me if she had diabetes.

'Have you lost weight?' I asked her.

'No. I've been dieting but I haven't lost any weight yet.'

'Do you feel unusually thirsty?'

'No.'

'Are you always hungry?'

'No, not more than usual. I've always had a good appetite.'

'Do you pass urine more often than usual?'

She thought for a moment. 'No.'

'Any tingling or numbness in your hands or feet? Do you find that bruises take a long time to heal?'

'No, no, not at all.'

'Have you been more tired than usual?'

'No, I don't think so. I feel tired now but I didn't sleep much last night.'

It seemed that I could rule out diabetes. But I still made a mental note to do a urine test nevertheless.

An overactive thyroid gland can cause excessive sweating and that can result in an unpleasant body odour. But patients with an overactive thyroid aren't difficult to diagnose. They are usually underweight, nervous and twitchy. Even if they don't have visibly enlarged thyroid glands or the slightly bulbous eyes which are classical symptoms of thyrotoxicosis they don't smell of fish. Still, I had to check.

'Have you been unusually nervous or restless?'

'No.'

'Hold out your hands for me, please.'

She held out her hands. There was no tremor, a common sign with thyrotoxic patients. I took her pulse which was absolutely regular, though a little fast.

I didn't think she had a thyroid problem.

I knew that malfunctioning kidneys could result in a build-up of toxins, and that a liver which wasn't working properly could do the same.

'Have you been short of breath? Nauseous? Any pains anywhere?'

'No.'

'Do your ankles well?'

'No.' She paused and thought for a moment. 'I suppose they do a little bit in the very hot weather. But they've always done that.'

'You don't feel tired all the time?'

'No. I was feeling fine until yesterday evening.'

'And you pass the usual amount of urine?'

'Oh yes.'

I leant forward and looked at her eyes carefully. There was no yellowing of her sclera. 'What colour is your urine? Is it darker than usual?'

'It's just the usual colour.'

'And your faeces – are they the usual colour?'

She looked puzzled. 'The what, doctor?'

'Your stools, when you open your bowels. Any change in colour?'

She looked a trifle embarrassed though whether this was because of the question or her original failure to understand I didn't know. 'Oh, no, nothing unusual.'

'And your periods are normal?' I asked.

Mrs Manders was far too young to be going through the menopause but I had to ask because odd things do happen. And during the menopause there can be an increase in sweat production and a change in body odour. There can also be a change in the acidity of the vagina – leading to a change in vaginal odour.

'They're as regular as clockwork.'

'You have no trouble with incontinence?' I asked. Urinary incontinence is uncommon in young women. But, again, I had to ask.

'Oh no,' she replied.

I had now pretty well run out of questions.

It is surprising how much you can learn simply by asking questions.

Lots of big city doctors have a tendency to send their patients off for loads of blood tests, X-rays and so on when they're trying to make a diagnosis. But for country doctors this can take a lot of time and be very inconvenient for patients. So I always preferred to find out as much as I could by asking questions.

'I want to test a sample of your urine,' I told her. 'Normally, I'd ask you to pop into our loo and pee into a bottle for me. But I need you to go home and have a bath and remove all your perfume so I'll give you a bottle and you can take it home with you. I'll call in and see you this afternoon and I can do the test then.' I took a sample bottle out of a tray on the trolley behind me and handed it to her.

I had another reason for doing this. In order to reach our loo, Mrs Manders would have to go through the waiting room and I knew that she wouldn't want to do this with her face still streaked with tears and her make-up looking awful. She'd already suffered enough embarrassment. It would save her two trips through the waiting room if I let her leave my consulting room through the French windows.

'You want to see if I smell?' she asked.

'Of course,' I replied.

She nodded.

I'd asked a lot of questions but I'd got nowhere near to making a diagnosis that would take me any closer to finding a solution to Mrs Manders's problem. I had to know what she smelt like.

I let her out through the French windows and rang for the next patient.

It was just before three o'clock that afternoon before I rang the doorbell at Mrs Manders's home. To my surprise, her husband Gerald answered the door. He didn't invite me in straight away but stood on the doorstep.

'I came home at lunchtime and took the rest of the day off,' he explained. 'She was so upset that I wanted to stay at home this morning but she told me that there was nothing I could do and that I should go to work.'

'But you've been worried all morning?'

He nodded. It was clear from his eyes that he too had been crying. 'I hate to see her like this,' he said. 'How could anyone have been so cruel?'

'The manager?'

'Yes. He broke her, doctor. She's usually a strong woman but even if it had to be said he didn't have to say it like that, did he?'

It occurred to me that Mr Manders was trying to tell me something.

'She's always been a good employee,' he said. 'She often worked extra hours and did more Saturdays than anyone else.'

'Have you noticed something?' I asked him.

'Maybe,' he said. 'Just a little bit.'

'For how long?'

'For a month or maybe six weeks at most. But I didn't say anything.'

'Has it been getting worse?'

'No, not really. No, I don't think so. She wears a lot of perfume but I can still smell something odd.'

'How would you describe it?'

'Not very pleasant,' he said. 'Sort of rotten eggs and a garbage sort of smell more than just fishy like they said.'

'Not very nice?'

He looked over his shoulder, obviously looking to see if his wife could overhear him. 'No,' he agreed. 'Not very nice.'

'But you didn't say anything?'

'No, of course not. How on earth do you tell someone you love that they smell a bit funny?'

It was a good question.

'Where is she?'

'She's upstairs in the bedroom. She was in the bath for over an hour.'

'Can I go up?'

'Of course.'

He stood aside so that I could go past him into the house.

Mrs Manders was sitting in a chair in their bedroom. She was wearing a nightie with a dressing gown on top of it. She had clearly been crying again. As I approached her she pointed to the sample bottle I had given her. It was standing on her dressing table. 'I've done the sample, you wanted.'

'Well, let's test that first,' I said. I was desperately hoping that I'd find something that would give me a clue.

I don't think I have ever before hoped to find a sign of a problem when testing a patient's urine but this time I was hoping that I would either find a sign of an infection or maybe clear evidence of sugar in the urine.

I took a testing strip from a bottle in my black bag and checked the urine.

It was absolutely normal. There wasn't any sign of any abnormality at all.

'Have you found anything, doctor?' asked her husband who had followed me into the bedroom.

'It's perfectly fine,' I told him.

'Nothing wrong?' asked Mrs Manders, and it was clear that she too had been hoping that I would find some abnormality.

'No. There's nothing wrong.'

I moved across the room and sat on the end of the bed so that I was only a couple of feet from Mrs Manders.

And now I knew that we really did have a problem.

There was a faint smell of soap but the overpowering smell was one of a mixture of rotten eggs and rotting fish.

'Can you smell anything?' whispered Mrs Manders.

I nodded. What else could I do? There was absolutely no point in my denying that there was a problem.

Mrs Manders started to cry.

'We'll find out what it is and deal with it,' I told her. I then asked her to lie down on the bed so that I could examine her. Tactfully, Mr Manders excused himself and left the bedroom. I heard him clatter down the stairs.

Fifteen minutes later, after I had checked her heart, her lungs, her abdomen, her limbs and everything else I had found absolutely nothing wrong with her. I would have given her a completely clean bill of health if I'd been performing the strictest of health insurance examinations.

'Has your diet changed at all recently?' I asked her, suddenly wondering if the smell might be caused by something she was eating. Eating asparagus, for example, can cause a dramatic change in the way a body smells – and, in particular, in the way that urine smells.

'No,' she replied.

'You aren't eating anything different? You haven't started eating a food you've never eaten before?'

'No.'

'Am I right in thinking that you don't want to go back to work?'

She shook her head vigorously. 'I could never go back there,' she said.

I took a pad of sick notes out of my black bag, wrote one out and handed it to her. 'I've put you down as having a bad throat,' I told her.

She thanked me and put the sick note on the bedside table.

'I don't know what is causing your problem,' I told her. 'I can find absolutely nothing wrong with you. In fact, you seem to be in perfect health. But this evening I will do some research and I'll telephone you as soon as I know anything.'

'Do you think you'll be able to do something about it?'

'I'll do something about it,' I told her.

I never like making promises to patients but it seemed that there had to be a cause for Mrs Manders's problem and, if there was a cause, there had to be a solution. She was, or appeared to be, a perfectly healthy woman.

That evening, after my surgery, I sat down beside the fire with a pile of medical textbooks on one side of me and a pile of medical journals on the other side. Because we lived miles from any medical library, I kept all the journals to which I subscribed and I had built up my own small but quite comprehensive library.

'What are you looking for?' asked Patsy, as I flicked through one journal after another.

I told her.

'Oh the poor woman!' said Patsy. 'How could that manager have been so damned thoughtless and cruel? Surely he could have found a better way to tell her.'

'You would think so, wouldn't you?' I said. 'But when you stop and think about it what on earth do you say to someone in those circumstances? Her husband noticed the smell but he didn't say anything because he couldn't think of what to say or how to say it.'

'I suppose you could criticise him as much for not saying something as you can criticise the shop manager for saying something,' said Patsy. 'Crumbs, what a horrid dilemma. Can I help you? What are you looking for?'

'I don't know,' I admitted. 'I'm hoping I can find a disease that causes a nasty smell. Maybe there's a paper in a medical journal that will help.'

So for an hour or so we ploughed our way through the books and journals.

'Are you looking for anything that can cause a funny smell?' asked Patsy.

'Yes. Have you found something?'

'There's a short piece in this journal,' said Patsy. 'It was published a year or two ago, back in 1972.'

She handed me the journal, opened at the page where she'd found a short abstract of a paper published in an unusual American medical journal. The paper dealt with a substance called trimethylaminuria – something I'd never heard of – and referred back to another paper published just a year or so previously.

'All this was published after I'd qualified,' I said.

I tried to keep up-to-date by regularly reading medical journals and new textbooks but it's impossible for one doctor to keep up with all the new research published around the world. And I had definitely missed this piece of research.

The abstract I read had a short list of references attached to it – these gave the details of three scientific papers which dealt with the problem in more detail. The description of the disease exactly matched Mrs Manders's symptoms.

I looked at the clock on the mantelpiece. It was twenty past ten.

'I'm going to telephone Mrs Manders,' I said, getting up and heading for my surgery. It seemed to me that although it was late she and her husband would want to know my news sooner rather than later.

It was Gerald Manders who answered the telephone. He sounded short-tempered, even angry, at being disturbed. I told him who it was, apologised for calling so late and asked if I could speak to his wife.

'I think I've found the cause of your problem,' I told Mrs Manders. 'If I'm right, and I think I am, then you have a rare condition called trimethylaminuria.'

'What's that?'

'It's a metabolic condition which has developed because your body is unable to break down some substances which contain nitrogen and which are in the food you eat. One of the compounds is called trimethyalmine.'

'Can you cure it? Can you make it go away?'

'I don't know how to do that yet,' I told her. 'But there are some more scientific papers I need to study. Tomorrow morning I will telephone a big medical library in London and I should have the information I need the day after that.'

'Is it a dangerous disease?'

'No, I don't think so. It results in an unpleasant odour but nothing else. It isn't going to affect the functioning of your body's organs or threaten your long-term health.

'But do you think you'll be able to stop it making me smell badly?'

'I believe so,' I told her.

'What made it start?' she asked. 'I haven't changed my diet.'

'I don't know that,' I told her. 'Look, I just wanted to ring you to let you know that I now have an idea of what is causing your problem. I wanted to share my hope with you. I'll ring you in two days when the postman brings these papers I need to look at.'

'I'm very grateful,' said Mrs Manders.

And then she started crying again. A moment later I heard her husband's voice. He apologised for his brusqueness, thanked me for calling and asked me what I had found.

I told him what I'd told his wife. And I repeated that I would telephone when I had more news to tell them.

The following morning I telephoned a big medical library in London, spoke to one of the librarians and arranged for them to post me copies of the scientific papers I needed to read. I hadn't even heard of the obscure journals which had published the papers but, fortunately, the library had subscribed to them and was able to promise to send me what I needed in that day's post.

The day after that, when I'd read the papers I had been sent, I telephoned Mrs Manders again and told her that I'd go round to see her that afternoon.

'Trimethylamine has an extremely unpleasant smell, reminiscent of fish and rotten eggs, and it's produced in the intestines when certain types of food are eaten,' I explained. 'Normally, the trimethylamine is dealt with by the body. But when things go slightly wrong with the metabolic processes the trimethyalmine accumulates and is released in the sweat, the urine and the breath. For some reason this condition seems to affect women more than men. One expert has suggested that might be because the different hormones in women's bodies might aggravate the symptoms.'

'Is his trimethylwhatsit catching? Will my husband develop it?'

'No, definitely not. It's not infectious or contagious.' I wrote the name of the condition down on a piece of paper and handed it to her.

'But what has suddenly caused this to happen?' asked Mr Manders. 'Or is that a stupid question?'

'It's a very sensible question,' I told him. 'The theory seems to be that it is caused by changes to a gene in the sufferer's body. It's very rare and it's something that appears to be inherited.'

'Is there a remedy?' asked Mrs Manders. 'Is there anything you can give me?'

'I'll come onto that in a moment,' I said. 'But there are things that you can do to help yourself and they may be more important than anything I can do. First, you need to avoid too much stress or exercise – anything that makes you sweat.'

'Sweating can make it worse?'

'It can.'

'Then that's probably why it got worse in the shop,' said Mrs Manders. 'A couple of the other assistants had complained of the cold and so the manager had increased the heating and put up the temperature. They liked it hot but I did find it uncomfortable.'

'And you were sweating?'

She nodded.

'Second,' I said, 'I think you should stop taking the contraceptive pill. We'll need to discuss some other form of contraception for you.'

'Well, I'm not going back to work and so once this problem is sorted maybe we can think about starting a family,' said Mrs Manders.

'Let's try to get this under control first of all,' I suggested.

'Do you think that the contraceptive pill has caused the problem?' asked her husband.

'It might have made it worse,' I explained. 'If the condition is related to hormone levels then taking the pill would change those levels and might exacerbate the problem.'

'So stopping the contraceptive pill would help?'

'I think it could.'

'Is there anything else I can do?'

'Definitely. I think you could try cutting out the sort of foods that contain trimethylamine.'

'What are those?'

'I've made a list for you,' I told her. 'Eggs, milk, liver, kidneys, beans, peas, peanuts, cabbage, cauliflower, Brussels sprouts and broccoli. Oh, and seafood and shellfish.'

'Seafood?'

'It apparently contains trimethyamine,' I agreed.

Mrs Manders looked at her husband. 'When you asked me if my diet had changed I forgot about that,' she said. 'My brother recently started to work at a fishmonger in Ilfracombe. He's been bringing us mackerel, crab and other fish and shellfish and so we've been eating more seafood than before.'

'I'm afraid that you should probably cut fish out for the time being,' I suggested.

It was beginning to sound as if we had encountered a perfect storm; a cornucopia of circumstances just right for this condition to become apparent.

'You said there was also something you could probably recommend as a medicine,' Mr Manders reminded me.

'There are a few things we could try,' I said. 'But to start with I suggest that you try taking something called activated charcoal. I don't have any in the pharmacy at Bilbury Grange but you can buy it over the counter at chemists and health food shops. Taking vitamin B2 supplement might also help because vitamin B2 seems to help break down trimethylamine in the body.'

'You really think that all this will help?'

'I definitely do,' I said. 'Both the charcoal and the vitamin B2 It should help by decreasing the concentration of trimethylamine in the body. It seems that charcoal might help by converting the trimethylamine into something that is harmless and doesn't smell.'

'And all this is very rare, did you say?' asked Mr Manders.

'It is. In fact the condition was only first reported a couple of years ago. Before that no one knew it existed.'

'So if I'd come to you with this problem five years ago you wouldn't have heard of it?'

'No. To be honest I hadn't heard of it anyway until a couple of nights ago. But five years ago no one else would have heard of it either because no one had discovered it.'

When I left their home both Mr and Mrs Manders looked happier than they had done for days. They had quite a few things to try and I was quietly confident that the approach would work.

Happily, my confidence was well placed.

Within a week Mrs Manders was back in the surgery to tell me that her husband had told her that the unpleasant smell which had caused so much distress had now gone completely.

'I haven't put on any perfume today,' she said. 'Please tell me if you can smell anything unpleasant.' She stood just a couple of feet away from me.

I sniffed.

It seemed a rather rude thing to do but what alternative was there?

'Perfect!' I told her quite honestly. 'You smell as fresh as a spring garden.'

With a big, beaming smile she told me that for two days she and her husband had talked of leaving North Devon and going to live in another part of the country.

'To be honest I was terrified of going back into Barnstaple and seeing any of the other girls working in the shop – let alone the manager. But eventually we decided that it was silly to run away. I don't have to go into Barnstaple much anyway. I can do most of my shopping at Peter Marshall's shop and if we need anything else that has to come from Barnstaple then my husband can collect it – or we can go to Taunton instead.'

I told her that I was very glad that they had both decided to stay in the village and added that Peter would undoubtedly be delighted!

After the evening surgery I told Patsy just how valuable her detective work had been.

She looked at me. 'I've been meaning to ask you this since you first told me about this disease. Do I smell at all funny?'

'No. Definitely not.'

'Do you promise?'

'I promise. Do I smell funny?'

'Well, I didn't like to say anything…'

'But?'

'You do smell of bonfire a lot of the time.'

Mrs Manders's problem wasn't a laughing problem but I had to smile. Sometimes it is too easy to allow a patient's problem to get into your mind, dampen your spirit and poison your soul. A little black humour is sometimes an essential part of the armoury of a doctor and his nearest and dearest.

'I don't think there's a cure for that,' I said. 'I can't possibly stop having bonfires.'

'I didn't think you could,' said Patsy.

The Flagpole

I don't think I have yet mentioned how we came to have a flagpole decorating our garden.

Well, the whole flagpole thing was Patchy Fogg's fault

Patchy and I were at an auction in South Molton when he noticed that there was a flagpole for sale.

'You should buy that,' he said. 'It would look good in your garden.'

Naturally, I told him not to be daft, that I didn't want a flagpole, particularly not one that was 30 feet tall. 'I've got absolutely no intention of buying a flagpole,' I insisted. I continued to rummage through a large box of old books that was almost certain to be knocked down for 50 pence. Hardly anyone ever wants to buy the mixed box of books at a country auction but there are always some fascinating finds to be found therein. In among the Victorian novels by long forgotten authors and the inevitable farming Almanacs (full of remarkably dull and completely out-of-date stuff about crop yields and weather) and out-of-date books on mechanical engineering (full of incomprehensible diagrams of cogs and flywheels) there will invariably be a few bound volumes of old *Punch* magazine, *Windsor Magazine*, *The Captain*, *The Strand* and so on. These old volumes make marvellous reading.

'Your lot is up now,' said Patchy, nudging me as I continued to rummage.

I leapt to my feet, thrust my hand in the air and kept it there. I have never mastered the business of rubbing my nose, winking or tugging on an ear lobe – the little visual ticks which seem so popular among the professional dealers who dominate most auction rooms.

And two and a half minutes later I found myself being congratulated by Patchy on having purchased my very own flagpole for £4 excluding commission.

'I thought I was bidding for this box of books!'

'Haven't I always told you that you should pay more attention when you stick your hand up at an auction?' asked Patchy, whom I had until then always thought of as a good and dear friend.

'How on earth am I going to get a flagpole home?'

'Oh, don't worry about that. We'll tie it to the top of the van. It's an absolute bargain at £4. It would have cost twenty times as much if you'd bought it new.'

We tied the flagpole to the roof of Patchy's van and got the darned thing back to Bilbury Grange safely eventually, though we agreed that it was a good job we didn't see any policemen on our way home. The pole, which was a solid piece of Douglas fir and far heavier than either of us had expected it to be, overhung both ends of the van by quite a few feet and although Patchy managed to find a couple of old rags to tie to the two ends, I feel sure that our journey home wasn't exactly legal. My mood wasn't lightened by the fact that I had been so busy berating Patchy for tricking me into buying the flagpole that I'd missed the box of books I'd coveted. The box had been knocked down to a farmer from Countisbury who had paid 25 pence for the whole lot and, judging by the way he tossed the box into the trailer on the back of his tractor, probably intended to use them as fire-lighters.

'It looks like a flagpole,' said Patsy, when we got home and lifted it off the top of Patchy's van. 'But it can't possibly be a flagpole because why would you buy a flagpole?'

'It's an absolute bargain!' Patchy said to her. 'You could sell this next week and make a profit.'

'Can't we sell it this week and just get whatever it was we paid for it?'

'It was only £4,' I pointed out, rather weakly using the traditional fact that it hadn't cost very much to justify having bought it. 'Plus commission.'

'The only other bidder was going to chop it up for firewood!' said Patchy. 'That would have been a crime.'

'It was a crime to buy it,' said Patsy. 'Where are we going to put it?'

'I thought we could put it up just down beyond the summerhouse,' I suggested. 'There's a big patch of grassland down there that needs livening up a little.'

'I'd rather thought of having a camellia bush there,' said Patsy.

'We can still have a camellia bush,' I pointed out. 'Maybe we should have two or three.'

'Did you get a hole and a flag with the flagpole?'

'A hole?'

'Well, presumably you can't just stand it up without putting one end into a hole.'

Patchy and I had, of course, completely forgotten that when you have a flagpole you need a hole to put it into and neither of us had expected that purchasing a suitable hole could prove to be considerably more difficult to organise, and more expensive, than buying the flagpole.

Who would have thought that a hole could cost so much?

Our first thought had been to bang in a fencepost (approximately the same width as the flag pole) and then use the grab on the back of a tractor to pull the fencepost out of the hole. We would then insert the flagpole into the empty hole.

That, at least, was our plan and it sounded easy so, naturally, it didn't work.

In the end we had to hire a specialist flag pole hole maker to come from somewhere up near Bristol. He made the hole, put in a special metal sleeve to protect the wood and to make sure that the flagpole didn't rot, and presented us with a bill that was so large that I am still too embarrassed to mention what it was. Patsy and I don't like to talk about it. All I can say is that I assume that the man who made the hole lives in a mansion and has loads of servants.

It was the flagpole hole borer, a weedy fellow with ginger hair who pointed out that if we wanted to fly a flag we would have to equip it with pulleys, clips, toggles and halyards and that it would be considerably easier to fix these essentials to the flagpole before we erected it. Fortunately, he happened to have all the necessary bits and pieces with him and was able and willing to sell these items to us at a very reasonable price. Since it seemed unlikely that Peter Marshall would have everything we required available in his shop we felt had little choice but to purchase what we needed there and then.

(Just for the record, it turned out that we were, of course, quite wrong about Peter Marshall's shop not having what we needed. I later discovered, purely by chance, that Peter had everything we needed in stock. Indeed, he had a surprisingly comprehensive supply of both new and second hand flagpole accessories. And he even had a flagpole for sale, though it wasn't quite as tall as the one I purchased. I learnt, once again, that one should never under-estimate the ability of a village shopkeeper to supply the unusual. Even more surprising was the fact that Peter's prices were considerably lower than the prices charged by the professional flagpole hole borer.)

Arranging for the man to come and make our hole took about a month. It seems that you can't just rush the business of having a hole bored for a flagpole.

But then, at long last, came the fun part: picking a flag, finding a way to fix it the halyard, and flying it!

Our first flag, purchased at Thumper Robinson's suggestion, was a Jolly Roger; a good old piratical skull and crossbones on a black background. We flew that flag for six months or so until the wind finally tore it to shreds.

'I liked the skull and crossbones,' said Patsy, as we contemplated a replacement. 'But now I fancy something a little more dignified as a replacement.'

(Patsy, I am pleased to say, had grown to like the idea of our having our own flagpole.)

We replaced the Jolly Roger with a traditional England flag – the one with the three golden lions, rampant on a maroon background, just as they are displayed on England cricket, rugby and soccer shirts.

The flag with the three lions goes back to the 12th century and predates the flag of St George, the familiar one showing a red cross on a white background. The cross of St George has only been used as an England flag since 1606 when it was used in the design of the Union Flag. (Some flag experts do say, however, that the red cross was used by English soldiers from the late 13th century onwards. This still means that the three lion flag is the original flag of England.)

It was Henry 1st (known as 'the lion of England') who first had a lion on his standard. He then added a second lion because his first wife had a lion on her family crest. Finally, he added a third lion because his second wife also had a lion on her standard.

Later, in the 12th century, Richard III (aka Richard the Lionheart) also adopted the three lion flag and it then became the official flag of England.

So that's the flag which we chose and which has, ever since then, flown on our flagpole.

Patsy agrees with me that it looks rather smart.

We leave the flag flying all the time, unlike a chap I know who has a union jack flying on a pole fixed on his front lawn. He takes his flag down on windy days because he says that it gets frayed when the wind blows and then has to be replaced too often. Personally, I can't see much point in flying a flag only on calm days but it was his flagpole and he was paying for the flags so I didn't say anything when he told me what he did.

Now, Patsy agrees with me that there is something wonderfully invigorating about watching a flag fully stretched in a high wind.

And so, all things considered, I have no doubt that sometime soon we will probably find it possible to forgive Patchy.

But not yet, of course.

I still have far too much fun seeing him squirm when I remind him (and anyone who is listening) of the day I wanted to buy a box of old books and ended up buying a flagpole.

The Painter

'I've developed this terrible trouble with my right arm,' said
Auberon Lambert, slumping down in the chair. He rubbed his right
hand and wrist with his left hand as he spoke.

Mr Lambert was a tall, slightly overweight, dignified looking man
in his middle fifties. He and his wife lived in the village before I
arrived but they were people who kept themselves to themselves. I
had never seen either of them in the Duck and Puddle, in the local
church or at any social events. I had seen Mrs Candida Lambert at
Peter Marshall's shop occasionally.

Mr Lambert was a painter. I knew of his reputation for he was
something of a local celebrity and his paintings of seascapes and of
wild moorland over Exmoor had won him many fans. Both Patsy
and I liked his work very much indeed and Patsy, in particular, was
hugely enthusiastic. A year or so earlier she had bought a print of
one of his paintings, a wonderful picture of a rocky cove called
Heddon's Mouth, and it hung in our drawing room.

'What sort of trouble? A pain? A weakness?'

'I don't really know how to describe it. There is some pain and
weakness and some numbness and some tingling too. And my grip is
weak. I've been dropping things. I can't extend my arm properly. I
can't straighten my wrist and fingers. It's all a devil of a nuisance.'

'Do you have the pain and the other symptoms only in your hand
and wrist?'

'No. The pain starts in my thumb, and the fingers next to it, my
index and middle fingers, but it goes up the underside of my arm and
seems to affect this muscle at the back of my upper arm. Not the
biceps muscle, the other one. I forget what it's called.'

'The big muscle at the back of your upper arm is your triceps.'

'That's the one,' he said. 'I should know that for heaven's sake. I
studied anatomy for long enough.'

'Why did you study anatomy?' I asked, slightly puzzled.

'I did it when I was at college. I spent three years studying art and we had to learn about the human body – bones, muscles and so on.'

'Of course. So the pain and tingling affect your hand, your wrist and your arm – all the way up to your triceps?'

'Yes, that's about it.'

'How long have you had the symptoms?'

'Just a couple of days. I left it yesterday because I thought the symptoms would just go away by themselves – as mysteriously as they arrived. But it's no better today than it was two days ago. It's no worse, but it's no better.

'It sounds as if it's your radial nerve that is affected.'

'Yes, I remember the radial nerve. It goes all the way up the arm doesn't it? I suppose it does sound as if that's the cause of the trouble. But, good heavens, how on earth have I damaged my radial nerve? Does this mean I'm always going to be like this?'

'I didn't say that you'd damaged it!' I said quickly. I had deliberately not used the word 'damaged'. 'The word damage suggests something that might be permanent or at the very least something serious. You can traumatise the nerve without damaging it. And sometimes the symptoms are very short lived.'

He looked extremely relieved.

'I'm a painter,' he explained. 'And at the moment I can't paint. I can't even hold a damned paint brush. And if I could hold a brush I wouldn't be able to control it properly.'

'Have you fallen or knocked your arm?' I asked.

He didn't have to think before replying. 'Neither,' he said.

'Have you been doing anything unusual? Working in the garden? Using a hammer? Digging? Using garden tools more than usual?'

He shook his head. 'I don't do any of that stuff. I'm afraid I'm utterly useless in the garden and I wouldn't know which end of a hammer to hold. My wife looks after the garden and if we need something doing around the house we call in a handyman.'

I nodded. His wife Candida Lambert had, over recent years, won numerous prizes in the various local flower and vegetable shows. Her Hollyhocks were said to be among the best in Devon, let alone North Devon. She sold quite a lot of her vegetables through Peter Marshall's shop and although Patsy and I grew most of our own vegetables, we sometimes bought stuff that she'd grown. Peter used to sell her vegetables from a separate box and he charged a little

81

more for them. Mrs Lambert seemed to have a knack with carrots and parsnips, and though she insisted that this was simply a consequence of having really suitable soil, I found this difficult to believe. It is difficult to grow root crops without them splitting or producing bifurcated tap roots. It is, in particular, easy to grow carrots and parsnips that taste rather woody. I've been told that it's a question of preparing the soil with the right amount of water and manure. Mrs Lambert always managed to grow vegetables which tasted as good as they looked.

'You haven't cut yourself?' I asked him.

He shook his head, pulled up his sleeve and held out his arm. There were no signs of any injury; no cuts and no bruises.

'Do you play any sport?'

'Chess. I play chess. But just with a chap I know who lives in Canada. We post each other our moves.'

'So it's hardly what you'd call a hectic activity?'

'I make about one move a fortnight. Our current game has been going on for eighteen months. Our last game lasted for two and a half years. The chap I play with is in his 80s and he's left instructions in his will that if he dies in the middle of a game then his moves should be completed by his son. It's not exactly a dangerously fast sport.'

'No other sports?'

'No. I walk around the village occasionally. But I'm not much of a walker I'm afraid. I only go out occasionally. We have a lovely cottage with a terrific view. To be honest, we don't go out much at all. We're rather reclusive.'

I nodded. Their home, which was called Woodworm Cottage, was one of the many small but beautiful cottages in the village. It had a thatched roof and a beautiful wooden porch. In the summer, pink climbing roses adorned the porch and the front of the house.

I had seen Mr Lambert walking around the village once or twice. He weighed several stone more than he should have done and if he were making a list of his favourite hobbies it was a reasonable guess that eating would be higher on the list than walking. 'Have you slept in a funny position at all recently?'

He frowned, seemingly rather puzzled. 'No,' he said.

'You haven't slept in a chair, for example?'

'Good heavens above! No! I haven't slept in a chair since I was a student. Why on earth do you ask me that?'

'Sometimes people fall asleep in a chair, with their arm hanging over the side or back of the chair. Their radial nerve gets temporarily crushed and they end up with the symptoms of nerve damage. It's only very temporary.'

'Ah. No. I definitely haven't slept in a chair.'

I was beginning to feel puzzled. I had excluded all the common causes of radial damage.

'I was getting rather desperate in my search for a cause. You can't really cure a medical problem like this without knowing why it has happened. I was beginning to wonder if the problem might not be a poisoning of some kind.

'Did the symptoms start suddenly or slowly?' I asked.

'Oh suddenly,' he replied. 'I woke up with them.'

'Your wife hasn't noticed any symptoms?'

'No. She is fine.'

'You don't have lead pipes in your cottage?'

'No. We had the cottage completely re-plumbed when we bought it. Actually, there really wasn't much in the way of plumbing. It was one of those cottages with just a cold tap in the kitchen and an outside loo. We had a bathroom put in upstairs and when we had the kitchen fitted out we had a proper sink with modern hot and cold taps. The piping is all that copper stuff.'

The beauty of old cottages is that you can do things like this to them. The walls of an old cottage tend to be thick enough and tough enough to handle some banging and hammering. If you tried to put new plumbing, fresh electrical wiring or central heating into a modern cardboard house the building would probably fall down at the very sight of a hammer. A relative of Patchy's, who lives near London, purchased a newly built home. He took down a thin, internal wall which was not a load bearing wall and the house developed some frightening cracks. Patchy said that the whole house darned near collapsed around him.

So it didn't seem as though Mr Lambert had been poisoned by lead in the drinking water. I flicked through his medical records envelope. There wasn't much in it. He'd broken his fibula playing football at the age of 16 and he'd had ringworm when he'd been in the army. Otherwise, he had enjoyed a very healthy life – until now. I put the medical records envelope down.

'Do you have any other illness or symptoms that I don't know about?'

'No. I'm lucky in that I have quite good health. I'm a bit overweight,' he said patting his tummy. 'But that's about it.'

I decided I'd better give him a pretty full examination. Diabetes and kidney disease can both cause inflammation and fluid retention which can lead to nerve compression. There were no signs of any fluid retention. But I had to check.

Twenty minutes later I was still no further forward. There were absolutely no signs of any problem with his kidneys and he definitely didn't have diabetes. His blood pressure was perfectly normal and I could find nothing wrong with his heart.

I was beginning to think that I would have to refer him to the hospital where they could do some tests on his nerves and muscles. At least the hospital would be able to organise some physiotherapy to help deal with the symptoms. Massage, physical therapy or even a splint can often prove helpful. The only thing I could think of for the moment was to prescribe a painkiller with an anti-inflammatory action. And the best drug available was aspirin – good, old-fashioned aspirin.

Many doctors didn't think much of aspirin because it wasn't new, it wasn't expensive and it wasn't heavily promoted by a drug company with a busy marketing department. There were many alternatives available but, taken in the soluble form, I still thought that aspirin was still the most effective and safest drug for the treatment of pain and inflammation.

And then suddenly, quite unexpectedly, a hint of a possibility of a clue appeared.

'All this couldn't have happened at a worse time,' he said. 'A week ago I started work on a new commission, something a bit outside my usual line, and now I can't work on it at all.'

'In what way is it different?' I asked him.

'I usually paint in a fairly loose, easy style,' he said. 'I suppose you could describe me as an impressionist.'

I smiled. 'I know your work,' I said. 'We have a print of one of your paintings hanging in our drawing room. It has pride of place.'

'Really? Which one?'

'I can't remember the name of it but it's a painting of Heddon's Mouth. It's a beautiful painting which shows the sea crashing over the rocks.'

'Ah, that one is called simply 'Heddon's Mouth',' said Mr Lambert. 'I can never think up clever titles. You were involved in an amazing rescue there a year or two back weren't you?'

'I was,' I agreed. 'A man slipped between two rocks and got stuck.'

'And the tide was coming in.'

I nodded.

I have to admit that just remembering that day made me shiver slightly. I had to amputate the man's leg so that we could drag him out from between the rocks.

'That was quite a rescue. The tide comes in very quickly along this bit of coast and Heddon's Mouth can be quite scary when it's windy. It was pretty rough that day, wasn't it? Candida's brother was down there fishing that day. He said it was quite an impressive rescue and he's not a bloke who is ever easily impressed.'

'Thank you,' I said, feeling slightly embarrassed and not really knowing what else to say. 'Let's get back to your painting. In what way is this new commission different to your usual work?'

'I usually sell my work through two galleries, one in Barnstaple and one in Exeter, and the owner of the gallery in Exeter recently put me in touch with a family in Exeter. The guy runs a factory, I can't remember what they make, and he wanted someone to paint a portrait of his extended family. You know the sort of thing, a big picture of all the family – including the children and the grandparents. Heaven knows why but they wanted it to be like one of those pictures Rembrandt used to do – with everyone standing in a line looking as if they've just had some really bad news.'

'I've never really been a huge fan of those formal pictures,' I said.

'Nor me,' said Mr Lambert. 'To be perfectly honest, paintings such as 'The Nightwatch', 'The Anatomy Lecture' and 'The Draper's Guild' always left me cold. I know I shouldn't say it but to me they always seemed to be nothing more than corporate portraits done to hang on the wall somewhere and impress visitors. Rembrandt also did family groups and they always looked to me to be a bit wooden. Rembrandt was a master but he was also the early forerunner of the family photographer – the chap who comes in and takes a picture of everyone looking at the camera and saying 'cheese'.'

I laughed. I felt the same way.

'Anyway, for some bizarre reason this chap in Exeter wanted me to paint the family members all in a line and to make it look like a photograph. He is apparently quite a rich fellow so he was prepared to pay a big fee for the painting. The gallery owner didn't know any portrait painters he could ask, most of the well-known ones seem to work in London, and he didn't want to lose his commission, so he asked me if I'd do it. I used to do a few portraits many years ago – before I found I was able to earn a decent living painting impressionist pictures of the sea and the countryside. So I agreed to do it. I took loads of Polaroid pictures and, as I say, I started work on the picture a week ago.'

'Presumably, you have to paint in a different style to do something like that?'

'Oh yes. My usual style of painting is very fluid, very easy.'

'And with this portrait? It's a very different way of painting?'

'Oh, yes, it's completely different; it's very precise, very accurate. Every tiny brush stroke has to be just right. I know a fellow in Yorkshire who does landscapes and he paints in every blade of grass and every leaf. When you look at one of his pictures you think you're looking at a photograph. I call it ultra-realism and to be honest I've never been a fan of that type of painting either. If you're going to paint something that looks like a photograph then why not just take a photograph?'

I smiled, and nodded for him to go on. I began to think that we might be getting close to an explanation.

'So I accepted the commission, purely out of greed I'm afraid.' He grinned. 'The fellow was prepared to pay a pretty huge fee for what he wanted.'

'And doing something like this completely changes the way you paint?'

'Oh yes, very much so.'

'You hold the brushes in a different way?'

'Definitely! My normal style of painting is, as I say, rather loose and fluid. But to do this sort of very realistic painting you have to grip the brush very tightly. Well, I do anyway. Other painters might do it differently but I found that I had to keep a really tight grip on the brush in order to get the precise sort of result that I need.'

'Are you finding it stressful to change your way of painting?'

'Massively. Absolutely massively. Candida didn't want me to take the commission. She said that she didn't see why I should accept it at all. I make enough money out of the sort of painting I do and Candida grows all our vegetables and makes a little more money by selling the surplus.'

'So when you started to do this portrait, you gripped the brushes very tightly and you were tense.'

'Yes, that's right.' He stopped for a moment. 'Oh, golly, I see what you mean! You think that in changing my style of painting I might have done something that caused this problem with my radial nerve.'

I nodded. 'Gripping anything very tightly can cause trauma to the muscles. Doing it while you're gripping something small, like a paint brush, can probably make it worse. And doing it for long periods is almost certain to cause problems. It can cause what's called a mononeuropathy, damage to a particular nerve – in your case the radial nerve.'

'Is the damage going to be permanent?' he asked anxiously.

'Certainly not! Take a few days off from painting to give your muscles a rest. The problems should disappear quite soon if you can stop gripping too tightly. And you need to put down your brushes every 15 to 20 minutes and make sure that the muscles are relaxed. Just massage them gently, or shake them as if you were trying to get rid of droplets of water. And it probably goes without saying that you need to try not to get so stressed about it all. To speed up the recovery I suggest you take a couple of soluble aspirin tablets every four hours.'

'And that's all?' That will do the trick?'

'Yes.'

'I won't need an operation?'

'Good heavens, no.'

I had never seen anyone with Mr Lambert's symptoms caused in this way. But I was confident that between us we had isolated the cause – and found the solution.

'And once the problem has gone I'll be able to go back to my normal style of painting?'

'Definitely.'

Mr Lambert took in a deep breath and let it out again quite quickly. He nodded at me, as if I'd just given him some valuable advice. 'I'm going to tell them I can't do this painting,' he said. 'I was a fool to take it on. It's not the sort of thing I like doing, it's not the sort of thing I want to do and it's probably not the sort of thing I'm best at.'

'Will that cause problems for you?'

'Oh no. I haven't been paid anything so I haven't got to give any money back. And the gallery owner will find someone else to do the painting. I've wasted a bit of time preparing the groundwork – the Polaroids and so on – but that doesn't matter and it's been a pretty valuable lesson. Mr Lambert suddenly looked considerably happier than he had when he'd entered the surgery. 'Once my radial nerve has recovered, I'll go back to painting my usual stuff.'

'I can give you a sick note if you like, confirming that this style of painting has created a real physical problem for you.'

'Could you do that?'

I nodded, scribbled out an appropriate note and handed it to him. He put the note into his pocket, stood up and gingerly offered me his other hand to shake.

'Give me a ring and let me know how things go,' I told him. 'It'll probably take a few days for the nerve and your muscles to settle down.'

When Mr Lambert left he was smiling. His physical symptoms weren't any better than they'd been when he came into the surgery. But I was confident that we had found the cause and he seemed very happy about the decision he'd made.

Mr Lambert didn't ring but three days later I got home from doing my afternoon calls and Patsy showed me a large parcel wrapped in brown paper that had been delivered.

'What on earth is that?' I asked.

'I haven't got the faintest. But Mr Lambert brought it round.

I carefully tore open the brown paper.

And inside, beautifully framed, was the original of the print we'd got hanging in our drawing room.

It was one of the nicest, unexpected and most welcome gifts I've ever received from a patient.

Card Skimming (1970s style)

Thumper Robinson and I were in the Duck and Puddle, sitting in our usual seats beside the fire. Frank Parsons, who was, with his wife Gilly, the co-proprietor of the pub and who was sitting with us, had positioned himself nearest to the fire so that he could keep the fire well fed. It is Frank's boast that no one goes hungry or cold in the Duck and Puddle. The new barman, Gengolphus 'Harry' Stottle (formerly known in London to his celebrity patients as psychiatrist Dr Pelham Ronald Eckersley but now known to one and all as 'Harry' the barman) was behind the bar, leaning on the counter and looking happier than I'd ever seen him look. And why shouldn't he look happy – he had in front of him a pint of Old Restoration, a huge ham and pickle sandwich on fresh, crusty white bread and an hour or so of stimulating conversation with the brightest brains for yards around.

As Harry himself once said: 'A man who isn't smiling when he has a pint of the best and a decent sandwich in front of him is clearly suffering from a serious malady affecting his body or his nature.' Harry it has to be admitted, was no advertisement for temperance or sobriety or, indeed, for political correctness.

Harry, now firmly settled in Bilbury and living in a cottage which he had rebuilt after a disastrous fire, had recently acquired a new cat which he had called Hardy. I had made the mistake of asking him 'Why?'

And Harry had explained that when Thomas Hardy died at the age of 87, his will had stated that he was to be buried at Stinsford in Dorset, a mile or so away from the town of Dorchester, unless the nation strongly desired otherwise, and required him to be buried in Poet's Corner in Westminster Abbey.

A compromise was reached.

It was decided, by the people who decide these sort of things, that Hardy's ashes would be interred at Westminster but that his heart would be buried in Stinsford. However, when the pathologist removed Hardy's heart in order to accommodate the unusual requirements of the nation's need for a double burial, the urn in which the heart was supposed to have been placed had not arrived.

'So the pathologist wrapped Hardy's heart in a tea towel and put it into a metal biscuit tin,' explained Harry. 'But, unfortunately, he didn't put the lid on properly. And when the undertaker entered the bedroom he found one of Hardy's pet cats sitting next to the open box and licking its lips. The heart, or most of it, had gone and was, it was safe to assume, was now tucked away inside the cat.'

'The undertaker, whose name was Charles Hannah, grabbed the cat, wrung its neck and put it in the urn with what was left of Hardy's heart. And then the heart, mostly now inside the cat, was placed into the polished wooden casket which was to be buried in Stinsford.'

'So that's why you called your cat Hardy?'

'It seemed as good a name as any and an excellent way to commemorate a wonderful and true story,' explained Harry with a shrug.

Like Harry, Thumper was also drinking a pint of Old Restoration. It had been his favourite beverage for a long time ('ever since man crawled out of the primordial soup', he once claimed in what was for him a rare foray into the world of academia) and if Frank served it in glasses big enough to hold a quart he would have drunk it from quart glasses to save time.

Frank himself was sipping a small whisky and water (Gilly Parsons, pleased with her husband's weight loss and my medical report on his blood pressure, which was now well under control, had recently increased his alcohol allowance to three single whiskies; one each on Tuesdays, Thursdays and Saturdays).

'Have you been down to Peter's shop lately?' Frank asked me.

'Not for three or four days.'

Peter Marshall, who runs the Bilbury village shop, was famous throughout North Devon for the slogan 'Buy One And Get What You Pay For', which was painted above his shop doorway, for the slogan 'Good things aren't cheap and cheap things aren't good' which he had embroidered on the breast pocket of the brown warehouseman's coat which he wore in the shop and for his numerous business plans.

'Oh, you should definitely go down and take a look,' said Frank.

'The caravan?' I asked.

'That's the one,' agreed Frank.

Peter had recently started something he called a 'time share' opportunity. Having read of developers who sold what they called 'time share' opportunities in Hawaii, Peter had decided to introduce the idea to North Devon. He had bought an old wreck of a caravan and instead of simply renting it out by the week to holidaymakers, he was selling shares in the caravan. Would-be holidaymakers could, for a sizeable sum of money, buy the right to spend a week in the caravan every year. Peter had bought a small advertisement in a magazine called *Exchange and Mart* and his promotional copy offered city-dwellers 'the chance to own their very own home in the country for a modest one-off payment'.

Peter once explained to me that any new and great enterprise requires two quite different human skills. First, it requires the vision, the imagination, to see an opportunity where no one else has seen one. Second, it requires a systematic, logical mind able to turn the dream into reality.

Peter modestly claimed to have both skills.

'How is the time share thing going?' asked Harry.

'The last I heard Peter had managed to sell 37 weeks,' I replied. 'I don't think the poor devils know what they've bought. Peter's advert was illustrated with a picture of the caravan lifted from the manufacturer's brochure. But the caravan they're buying has mould and leaks and looks as if it's been sitting in a field for a decade.'

'That'll be because it has been sitting in a field for a decade,' said Thumper. 'And it was pretty clapped out when it was dumped in the field.'

'Well the 'time share' project was last week's miracle business opportunity,' said Frank. 'He's now getting ready for Christmas.'

'But Christmas is weeks away!'

'Peter says that in the big towns they sell Christmas stuff in July.'

'Has he put up his decorations?'

'No, he hasn't done that yet. But he's got Christmas hampers for sale.'

'Hampers?'

'Well, that's what he calls them. He's selling old cardboard boxes filled with a variety of what he calls Christmassy items. The boxes he calls hampers have all got advertisements for soap powder printed on the side.'

'What sort of Christmassy items is he putting in them?'

'Well, for £5 you get a tin of baked beans, a tin of spaghetti hoops, three turnips, a bottle of beer, a bottle of lemonade, a tin of pilchards, a box of budgie seed, a little bell and mirror for hanging in your budgie cage, a small bottle of horseradish sauce, a large bottle of Tizer, a medium sized bottle of Vimto, and a standard sized bottle of Liebfraumilch. If you bought the £10 hamper you got all that lot plus a packet of Fisherman's Friend lozenges for coughs and sore throats, a bottle of anti-dandruff shampoo, a bottle of castor oil, a box of dates complete with a little, wooden fork, a bottle of antacid, a packet of aspirin tablets, a packet of custard, a two pound bag of caster sugar, an orange, a small bag of crystallised ginger, half a pound of butter, a two pound bag of mixed dried fruit, a sprig of plastic holly, a bag of flour, a bag of rice, a bottle of bleach and a packet of lemon puffs.'

'I thought a Christmas hamper was supposed to contain stuff like a Christmas pudding,' I said.

'I asked him about that. Peter said that his hamper has got all the ingredients to make your own Christmas pudding. He said that if you make your own pudding you'll feel a greater sense of pride than if you just buy the pudding ready-made.'

We sat and thought about this for a while. Peter never fails to surprise any of us.

Five minutes later Patchy arrived. He was walking slowly and clutching his head.

'What would you like to drink?' Harry asked him.

'I don't think I can manage anything alcoholic,' whispered Patchy. 'Adrienne and I had a romantic little dinner party to celebrate something. Don't ask me what because I can't remember. Adrienne bought a bottle of ouzo, that Greek stuff that tastes a bit like pastis and a bottle of brandy that she insisted had to be drunk immediately before it went bad. I drank too much of both and woke up with a hell of a hangover.'

Adrienne, who is Patchy's wife is also my sister-in-law. She used to be keen on natural remedies but had in recent years discovered that she preferred alcohol to herbal teas and liked to buy wines and spirits that no one had ever heard of but which seemed a bargain. As many people knew from bitter experience she believed that once a bottle had been opened the cork should be thrown away. No one could convince her that some varieties of alcohol, such as spirits, did not inevitably go 'off' and turn dangerous if not consumed within an hour of opening.

We had all looked at him, slightly shocked. It wasn't the fact that he had a hangover that was so surprising, but the fact that he appeared to be refusing an alcoholic drink. This was like a dog turning his nose up at a bone or a politician eschewing a photo opportunity.

'No hair of the dog?' asked Harry. 'What did you say you were drinking?'

It is widely believed, by those who drink alcohol with enthusiasm, that anyone who has imbibed too heavily can soothe their troubled body and spirit by drinking a glass of the same type of alcohol the morning after. The theory may sound self-serving but there is some historical basis for it. Both Hippocrates, the father of medicine, and modern homoeopaths believe that 'like cures like' and many historical figures (such as Rabelais) backed the notion of treating an ailment caused by one substance with a cure consisting of the same stuff. The expression comes from the idea of treating a bite from a rabid dog with a potion containing some of the dog's hair.

'I don't think I could cope with anything too alcoholic,' said Patchy. He held his head in his hands for a moment, as though checking to make sure that it was still there. 'Maybe I'll just have a glass of white wine,' he agreed, overcoming his reluctance with surprising speed. 'If that's what you all recommend. Maybe a large one would be better. Just leave the bottle.'

Harry removed the cork from a bottle of Patchy's favourite dry, white wine, poured a portion into one of the large glasses which are kept for his use and crunched the bottle down into an ice bucket, which he just happened to have prepared when he'd seen Patchy entering the bar.

I was nursing a glass containing a modest and entirely medicinal dose of Laphroaig malt whisky.

And, we all had one of Gilly's magnificent Duck and Puddle sandwiches before us.

In some hostelries where sandwiches are served, it is customary for the staff to serve a plateful of delicate little sandwiches, more suitable for photographing than for eating and adequate only for dainty nibbling by elegant ladies wearing white lace gloves. I have even heard of pubs and inns serving damp triangles of bread which were made a hundred miles away and which were served up enclosed in little, plastic containers. I shudder at the thought.

The Duck and Puddle's landlady much preferred to produce sandwiches which were meals in themselves. Indeed, Gilly's sandwiches always remind me of those magnificent doorstep sandwiches which the friendly wife of an innkeeper serves up to Robert Donat and Madeleine Carroll in Hitchock's original version of 'The Thirty Nine Steps'.

Moreover, Gilly usually served each sandwich with a large, pickled gherkin and a pickled egg.

The Earl of Sandwich himself could have sat on his horse, munched one of Gilly's magnificent creations and been well prepared for battle. My local dog Ben had, over the years, acquired a taste for a pickled gherkin and Gilly always put two gherkins onto my plate if Ben was with me, making it clear that there was one gherkin for me and one for Ben. 'She deserves one of her own,' Gilly would say, as Ben demolished the gherkin in a few happy bites.

As an aside, I should mention that a couple of days earlier a sales representative had called at the Duck and Puddle and had left behind, as samples, a selection of the new foods his company was offering for sale. These had, apparently, all been 'designed' by one of those famous television chefs who seem to think of food as gustatory wallpaper. There were half a dozen different types of flavoured crisps including: pickled shrimp with mustard; curried salmon with beetroot; mackerel and marmalade; lamb with paprika; beef and custard and mutton with peanut jelly. There were also some teacakes which contained bits of beetroot and radish. None of us had felt brave enough to test any of these items and so I had taken them all back to Bilbury Grange, emptied them out of their packets and offered them to Cedric, our pig. Cedric was never what you would call a picky eater but he rejected the whole kit and caboodle and I ended up having to put the lot onto our bonfire. I didn't even want to put them onto the compost heap.

As we ate our sandwiches, we ruminated on the history of the English public house. No one can possibly deny that the English have always been partial to a bevy or two, especially if accompanied by good food, all consumed in warm and congenial circumstances.

Our ruminations started when Frank raised his glass (happy that it contained something more spiritually enlivening than tonic water, his usual abstemious tipple) and suggested that we drank a toast to Jake Porter, a villager who had recently died.

Jake had been a mere stripling of 96 when he'd tottered off, exchanging his comfy fireside chair and harmonica for a fluffy, white cloud and a harp, and his early death had been something of a surprise to him and to all of us in the village. Both his parents and his brother had all received telegrams from Her Majesty the Queen congratulating them on reaching their centenaries. 'I'll reach 100 easily,' Jake had insisted at the celebrations for his 96th birthday. 'I've always had a full English breakfast, never smoked more than 40 a day and since I reached my 80th birthday, I've limited myself to half a bottle of whisky a day.'

When we'd drunk to Jake's memory, Patchy suggested that we drink to one another – wishing ourselves many years more in the comfort of the Duck and Puddle.

'Do you know where this habit started?' asked Harry.

We all looked at him. Harry is a mine of both useful and trivial information. You never know which sort you are going to get when he begins to tell a tale. And since he had started work as a barman, he'd been studying the history of drinking and of British public houses.

'What habit?' asked Thumper.

'Drinking a toast or pledge.'

We all thought for a moment, muttered various half-hearted nonsenses and then admitted that we didn't.

'It began in Saxon times,' said Harry. 'The Saxons were hard drinkers who enjoyed English ale and a glass of mead but they were always a bit nervous when knocking back a horn full of their favourite tipple.'

'Why a horn full?' asked Thumper.

'In those days, they drank from horns not glasses. Drinking glasses hadn't been invented.'

'Like a horn from an animal? A dead animal?'

'Exactly.'

'What the devil was mead?' asked Frank.

'A sort of beer sweetened with honey,' explained Harry, who was getting a little exasperated.

'I never knew that,' said Frank, surprised to discover that there was something about beer which he didn't know.

'May I continue?' asked Harry.

We all gave permission.

'The Saxons were always nervous when they drank,' continued Harry. 'They lived in fairly dangerous times and a bloke about to empty his horn would ask a pal to pledge him. The pal would then take out his sword, or his knife, and stand guard while the drinker took a good gulp of his mead, or whatever it was that was in his horn. Obviously, when a fellow was emptying his horn he couldn't look out for people creeping up on him, intent on stabbing him and robbing him, and so the pal who was guarding him helped make him feel safe. When the drinker had quenched his thirst he would then pledge or promise to stand guard while his pal took a slurp from his own horn. As the business of pledging became less necessary so drinkers simply got into the habit of drinking to each other's health.'

'Where the devil do you learn all this stuff?' demanded Thumper.

'Haven't the foggiest idea,' admitted Harry. 'I must have read it somewhere.'

We then segued comfortably into a discussion of the history of drinking and, more particularly, a history of English drinking establishments.

Harry explained that if you looked as far back in English history as the 10th century, you would discover that the English were such enthusiastic topers that King Edgar (who was known to his best chums as Edgar the Peaceful) felt he had to follow the advice of Dunstan, who was the Archbishop of Canterbury at the time, and close down a good many alehouses in an attempt to cut down the nation's drinking.

'Edgar decreed that there was to be only one alehouse per village,' said Harry. 'When that simply resulted in everyone piling into the one legally approved drinking place he ordained that pins or nails must be fixed into drinking horns at stated distances. Anyone who drank beyond the allowed mark could be punished.'

And, according to Harry, as the years tottered by, new rules were introduced to separate those establishments which catered to travellers and those which specialised in just providing drinks for the locals.

The former, those drinking places which specialised in looking after travellers, had to be open day or night, and they were known as inns while the latter, the places which only provided refreshments during the daytime, were known as taverns.

The inns weren't allowed to cater for locals who had just wandered in for a drink but they were legally bound to provide food and refreshment for any traveller – at whatever time of night they arrived.

The taverns were not allowed to accept overnight guests and had to close before midnight.

Over the years taverns became known as pubs and inns morphed into country hotels – though many still liked to describe themselves as inns. The drinking places which were classified as inns were usually smarter and a little more upmarket than taverns – which tended to cater to the local lowlife.

(Since the Duck and Puddle in Bilbury provides food, drink and overnight accommodation for travellers it is, strictly speaking, an inn rather than a pub. This means, of course, that it can provide refreshments for its bona fide guests at any hour of the day or night. Although this would not, of course, ever happen at the Duck and Puddle, where Frank, the landlord, has been described by his friends and drinking companions as both a paragon of virtue and a walking advertisement for probity, it is, from time to time, rumoured that country establishments may occasionally take advantage of the absence of immediate and local constabulary oversight to write the names of favoured regulars into the inn's official register of overnight guests. Those listed on the register as guests are, of course, entitled to purchase whatever refreshments they might feel appropriate. And, even in taverns, where there are no overnight guests, it is an open secret that if the doors are barred and shuttered at the official closing time then there is nothing to prevent the landlord from inviting friends to attend a private party, and to make merry for a little longer than the official opening hours might officially allow. This, I am told, is known as a 'lock in'. On Holy Island, otherwise known as Lindisfarne, it has been reputed that pubs stay open for an extra eight hours when the tidal causeway is flooded. Drinkers who are marooned on the island can imbibe for as long as they like as long as police officers, and those inclined to tittle-tattle, are all safely ensconced on the mainland.)

'Gradually, the traditional English inns acquired reputations for being the centre of their local community,' Harry continued. Once he warms to a theme it is nigh on impossible to deflect him. 'In addition to providing warmth, shelter, food and entertainment for travellers, local inns were often used as the local courtroom, the polling station and a meeting place for the local council.'

'We still do that,' said Frank. 'We were the village polling station at the last election and the council has often met here.'

Harry then explained that before the onset of the railways made travel comparatively easy, and relatively cheap, anyone who wandered more than 20 miles or so from home would need somewhere to stay and he would look for somewhere homely and welcoming.

'The average traveller wasn't interested in folderols,' said Harry. 'He just wanted a pint of something cheering, a bowl of good soup, a hunk of bread and a chunk of cheese. In those early days no one travelled for pleasure; they travelled because they had to.'

He told us that most people never left their home village and travellers were usually either pilgrims or salesmen (known as drummers). It is perhaps not surprising, therefore, that the oldest inns were called Pilgrims' Inns. And the posher inns, the ones where the landlord knew a word or two of French, were known as the local 'Maisons Dieu'.

'By the end of the 16th century, England's inns had never looked better,' continued Harry, who was clearly on something of a roll. 'And they had never provided their customers with better service or better fare. Many had tapestries on the walls and carpets on the floor and the food was invariably good to excellent. Popular dishes were brawn, neat's tongue, capon, goose, swan, venison, kid, hare, plover, snipe, larks, boar, sturgeon, crayfish, carp, pike, trout, elvers, lampreys, pigeons and rooks which were usually served in a pie. Popular puddings included saffron cake, gingerbread, marchpane, nectarines, custard, warden pie and olive pie. The customers drank sherris sack, malmsey, beer and a variety of wines which had been imported from France or Germany. A fairly ordinary meal in a travellers' inn would consist of eight or nine heavy courses. People ate a lot because there wasn't much to do apart from eat and drink. And travelling was hard work – If you wanted to get somewhere you either walked or you rode.'

'Wait, wait a minute!' interrupted Thumper. 'What on earth are elvers?'

'Baby eels.'

'And sherris sack? What is sherris sack?'

'Oh, that's just an old word for sherry.'

'And malmsey? I've always wondered what malmsey was.'

'Malmsey is madeira – a fortified white wine from the island of Madeira.'

'And what was marchpane?' asked Thumper.

'I know that one!' said Frank, to his own surprise. 'It's an old word for marzipan – almond paste.'

Harry then explained that by the 17th century, travellers could move about in coaches, and the inns where they stayed had become increasingly fancy.

'By the end of the 18th century, inns were offering previously unimaginable luxury,' he said. 'A traveller dining in a roadside inn would typically eat spitch-cocked eels, a whole roast pigeon, a loin of pork, a variety of tarts, jellies and custards and then finish with a few chunks of cheese.'

'Stop!' said Patchy. 'You've done it again. What the devil are spitch-cocked eels?'

'Eels cooked on a skewer.'

'What, like a kebab?'

'I suppose so,' agreed Harry.

According to Harry, coach and post-chaise travel was popular by the 19th century and so inns were crowded. They were still open 24 hours a day, of course, and the kitchen fire was never out. Travellers staying the night would expect to sleep in four poster beds. The beds would be equipped with curtains all the way round so that the maid or groom who came in to make up the coal fire, or bring in the tea and crumpets, couldn't see what was going on in the bed. Sirloin, mutton joints, Cheshire and Stilton cheeses were washed down with ale and travellers would expect to have a copy of *The Times* delivered with their breakfast. As inns competed with one another, meals got more and more extensive. A pretty ordinary meal for two would consist of a four pound turbot, two roast ducks, an apple pie and cheeses. Breakfast for two, served in the bedroom, would be cold ham and beef, Cambridge sausages and fried eggs, followed by a roast mallard. It was by no means unusual to have a tankard of ale with breakfast, and beer makers were experimenting with adding honey, yarrow, bog myrtle and ground ivy (nicknamed alehoof) to their brews.

Over the years, inns became an increasingly important part of English social life.

Oliver Cromwell and his officers began their plotting in a variety of pubs, including 'The Bear' in Cambridge, the 'Red Lion' in Barnet (where the future protector of England reported that he had eaten the best cheese cakes he'd ever tasted) and the 'George' at Norton St Philip. Admiral Horatio Nelson said goodbye to Emma Hamilton for the last time at the inn at Burford Bridge and Keats and Stevenson both wrote in the same establishment. Hazlitt and De Quincey both wrote their most famous lines in pubs, as did Charles Dickens. Indeed, Dickens was a huge fan of inns and many of his novels include vignettes of well-known taverns and inns. It is also now a matter of record that many newspapers were planned and put together on inn tables

In addition to being known for their food and drink, there is no doubt that English inns and taverns have always been places where sports and games could be played with great enthusiasm. Some of the favoured activities were, to say the least, a trifle on the esoteric side of eccentric. Apart from drinking and eating, people do all sorts of odd things in pubs – especially in country pubs which are, to a certain extent, a law unto themselves and which are quite unlike the pubs in towns and cities.

Urban folk usually went to their local public house because it was somewhere to drink and meet their pals. Pub customers drank, ate, chatted, smoked (if they were allowed to), made new friends, gossiped and flirted. To be honest there often wasn't much room for anything else because the pub owner, usually a large brewery or a company with a chain of similar establishments, had to cram in as many chairs and tables as it could in order to make the enterprise profitable.

The result was that in most town and city pubs the television set has taken over the task of providing entertainment, and the bar billiards table and dart board have been put down into the cellar to gather dust and cobwebs. Customers sat and drank their beer, munched their chicken in the basket or their scampi and chips or their bag of cheese and onion crisps, and they watched the football on the large-screen television set which was fastened high up on a wall and which dominated the room in every possible way. The only other source of entertainment was the local stripper who would usually have to climb onto a table to take off her clothes. There isn't room to do anything else – even if the customers had the inclination or the equipment. Worse still, was the fact that in large town pubs, the landlord and the bar staff were usually too busy for idle chatter and probably had too many customers to remember the names even of their regulars. There were, I'm pleased to say, many honourable exceptions but too many modern town and city public houses looked out-of-date the minute they'd been built; they were dull, uninviting and shabby. There was too much concrete outside and too much fake wood and red plastic inside. In the 1970s, there was an unforgiveable tendency for pub chains to equip their newly built premises with fake horse brasses and fake beams and to adorn the walls with cheap hunting prints.

Things were different in the countryside; in villages and hamlets such as Bilbury, pubs and inns such as the Duck and Puddle had for hundreds of years been the centre of the village. In small settlements, where there were no cinemas, theatres, bowling alleys or nightclubs the pub was all there was. It was a home from home and the village meeting place. Regulars had their own mug hanging over the bar and a chair by the fire that was respected as theirs every much as their own armchair at home was respected as theirs. In places of this ilk, the customers drank, ate, chatted and gossiped but they also played games. They played cribbage, poker, bridge and whist. They played shove h'penny and table skittles, dominoes, cribbage, pool, bar billiards and snooker.

And where there was enough room available (as there was in the Duck and Puddle, of course) they could play skittles – a sport which, when played the way it was played in English village pubs, was undoubtedly one of the most spectacularly dangerous of all sports whether played indoors or outdoors.

I knew from personal experience that a wildly thrown wooden bowling ball could do a good deal of damage to anything which got in its way. Skittles was the precursor of ten pin bowling but it was a much cruder, faster game and it caused far more injuries – largely because the spectators stood alongside the skittle alley and were therefore likely to be hit by balls which were misdirected or which bounced off the side boards or the skittles.

Where there wasn't enough room to play proper, old-fashioned skittles, the drinkers played a game called table skittles – which had the nine pins, or men, standing on a table or a board. A small wooden ball tied to a fixed stick was whirled around to knock down the pins.

Patchy said that table skittles was very popular in Northamptonshire where the table upon which the pins were stood had a leather padded back and sides and the skittles were knocked down with wooden disks called 'cheeses' which were skimmed at the target. Patchy said he'd seen it played and it was pretty deadly. 'Woe betide anyone who got in the way of one of the skimming 'cheeses'!'

Egg dancing was another sport which was popular in country inns. A dozen eggs would be laid out on the floor and a dancer would be blindfolded and told to perform a hornpipe jig without treading on any of the eggs. Bystanders would bet on how many eggs he would crush. Daft dances like this were very popular and could be extremely profitable. Men who could dance well were often rewarded with quite generous tips by rich publicans or benefactors – especially if they had helped someone win a large bet.

People danced on ropes too. In 1547, when King Edward VI rode through the city of London prior to his coronation, a rope was stretched from the battlements of St Paul's to an anchorage point in front of the Deans Gate house. When his Majesty was seen approaching a Frenchman, imported especially for the occasion, slid down the cable. He was lying down, with his head forwards and his arms and legs spread as though he were flying. When he had landed, he kissed the King's foot and then walked back up the cable and did a variety of tricks upon it. This sort of thing was quite popular and innkeepers would organise their own variations. Sadly, inevitably, things didn't always go as perfectly as planned. A later exponent of the sliding down the cable trick lost a leg. Undaunted, he had a false leg made out of wood and filled with lead so that it weighed pretty much the same as his real leg and wouldn't unbalance him. He went one further than the Frenchman because he carried a pistol in each hand and discharged them both as he came down the rope.

The imagination of performers and innkeepers seemed inexhaustible.

In one pub in Devon an acrobat, whose party trick was to hang from a beam by his toes, couldn't get down. He went black in the face and died because onlookers, all cheering merrily, thought the whole thing was just part of his act. A pub in North Devon once ran an Indoor Olympics Event which involved some very strange events. Contestants had to try jumping backwards up onto a mantelpiece (a favourite party trick of Corinthian C.B.Fry when he was over 70-years-old); kicking as high as they could manage (to leave a shoe mark on a white board) and performing a standing broad jump (the competitor stood perfectly still at a setting off point and had to jump as far as he could).

All this stuff was told to us by Harry who seemed to me to know enough about old pubs and inns and taverns to write a book about them.

At the Duck and Puddle we had, of course, always taken the game of darts quite seriously and over the years we've had a number of top players representing the club in county games. But history shows that darts was very nearly banned as a sport.

Harry explained that in 1908 the authorities in Leeds wanted to have the game banned because they said it was a game of chance and that those who played it were gambling. A player called Mr Annakin, who had a pub in Yorkshire, went to court to defend his sport. He played a court clerk who had never played the game before and thrashed him. After Mr Annakin had thrown three 20s for a score of 60, the clerk missed the board completely. The magistrate then insisted on having a go himself. He too missed the board. And so the court had no choice but to conclude that darts is not a game of chance but a game of skill.

The English love inventing games and, as a nation, have undoubtedly invented more games than any other people. It is actually quite difficult to think of a game that wasn't invented by an Englishman. Sadly, of course, the English usually turn out to be far better at inventing games than at playing them.

On the day of which I am writing we had all recently started playing a game which involved skimming a playing card into a hat. I have no idea who thought up the game but the rules were quite simple. A hat, usually my brown Fedora which had the widest brim of any of the hats we had available, was placed on a table and each player would stand five feet away with a full pack of 52 playing cards. The game would be to skim the cards, as one might do when skimming a flat pebble on a lake, so that they landed in the hat. A card which landed inside the hat scored one point. A card which landed on the brim of the hat, and stayed there, scored half a point. A card which missed the hat completely scored no points whatsoever. When one player had used all his cards his score would be recorded (usually on a beer mat), the cards would be collected up and the next player would take his turn.

For a while, we had experimented with scoring points according to the number of pips on a card. So, if the seven of hearts landed in the hat then the player would score seven points. If the three of clubs landed in the hat the player would score three points. If the eight of spades landed on the brim, the player would score four points. We gave up this version of the game because the scoring proved far too difficult.

We had finished our sandwiches and were busy playing our new game when two newcomers walked in. Judging by their boots, anoraks, haversacks and thumb sticks they were hikers and they both appeared to be in their 30s. Their gear looked expensive and brand new. Their thumb sticks bore little brass plates bearing the name of the maker and had clearly been purchased from an expensive store. I always think it's rather a pity that people buy walking sticks in preference to making their own. All you need is a stick and a penknife. If you want a fancy top for the stick, but don't want to carve your own then you can easily buy what you need. If you want a ferrule, whether metal or rubber, you can usually find what you need without too much difficulty. Peter Marshall's shop always sold ferrules and stick tops.

The distaff half of the pair was tall and slim and had obviously had her hair cut somewhere other than North Devon. Though perfectly competent with a pair of scissors, the woman who had taken over the hair dressing franchise in the hut next to Peter Marshall's shop had a limited repertoire of styles.

Similarly, I thought it fair to bet that her companion, the spear side of the duo, had been snipped and shampooed somewhere other than in North Devon. The chap whom I usually visited when my hair required trimming was a pleasant fellow, and on both of the occasions when he'd cut one of my ears he had apologised, but he had but two styles to offer: 'a light trim' and 'the military option'. This haircut was neither.

And judging by the map one of them was holding, not to mention the rather concerned looks on their faces, they were lost.

It is easy to get lost in Devon, very easy to get lost in North Devon and very, very easy to get lost in the lanes and on the footpaths and bridle paths of Bilbury.

Harry, relishing his new role as 'mine host', greeted the pair cheerily, looked at their map and told them where they were. They seemed surprised, apparently having thought themselves to be approximately 12 miles away to the East. He then complied with their orders by serving them one glass of tomato juice, one glass of lemon barley water and two packets of salt and vinegar crisps. They had asked for 'something organic in the snack line' but, sadly, Harry had had to disappoint them. Frank did mutter something about it being a pity that the curried salmon and beetroot crisps were no longer available. They were both exceedingly slim and it wasn't difficult to see why. If you've walked for half a day across the Devon moors and all you eat is a packet of crisps then your calorie intake is clearly not going to be excessive.

The hikers seemed intrigued by the game which we were playing.

'What's the game you're playing? What are the rules?' asked the male half of the couple, when he'd finished his lemon barley and eaten his crisps. He ate the crisps daintily, one at a time.

I couldn't help looking at Thumper when I saw the way the visitor was eating his crisps. Thumper's method of eating crisps is quite different. He pours the packet of crisps into the palm of his left hand, transfers the contents of his palm into his mouth and then crunches for about a minute before swallowing. We measured him once. He managed to get rid of a packet of cheese and onion crisps in 49 seconds flat. When I asked Thumper why he ate crisps so quickly, he explained that he always wanted to get back to the serious business of drinking his beer. Thumper had clearly also seen the way that the newcomer had eaten his crisps and had been rather hypnotised by the sight.

When he'd finished them, the stranger asked Harry if it would be all right if he put the empty packet into the fire. Harry said he thought it probably would be.

Patchy, whose turn it was to skim or flick the cards, explained the rules to the visitors.

'It's more difficult than it looks,' said Frank. 'If you aren't careful the cards tend to skim off the brim of the hat and land on the floor. You have to get them just right if you want them to land in the hat and stay there.' He explained how the secret of the game lay in the way that the card was flicked. 'It's all in the wrist movement,' he told them.

When we had finished the game, Patchy had scored 32, Thumper had managed 37 and a half, Frank had scored 18, Harry had scored 29 and I had scored a rather disappointing 25 and a half. I can usually do better than that but I always do badly when there's an audience. I'd have made a useless sports professional. Thumper picked up the 50 pence he'd won. (We had all put down a 10 pence stake.)

'It looks great fun!' said the woman.

'Don't be fooled by how easy we make it look!' said Frank.

'We've been playing for a week or two now,' I explained, preparing her for disappointment.

'The doc has written to the people who organise the Olympics suggesting that skimming cards into a hat be made an Olympic sport,' said Thumper, nodding in my direction to indicate that I was the one responsible for this. 'The game is more entertaining than synchronised swimming, requires more skill than weight lifting and is extremely adaptable.' he explained.

'It can be played by men and women,' I added. 'And you can play it indoors or, if the weather is good and there is no wind, you can even play outdoors. We don't think there is much chance of competitors doping themselves. I can't think of any drugs that would prove useful. We're rather hoping that the Olympics Committee might regard this as a plus point.

'The cards can carry advertising so there are immense commercial possibilities,' said Frank, who was clearly rather hoping that the newcomers might turn out to be associated with some company which would take up the game and make us all rich. 'I think we could easily make card skimming extremely attractive to money motivated organisations.'

'Would you like to try?' Patchy asked the newcomers. 'We won't expect you to put money on the table. Just try it for fun.'

The man said he didn't think he would bother, thank you very much, but the woman said she'd like to have a go – just for fun.

Patchy patted the cards together and handed them to her. She took them, looked at them, rather critically I thought, and then positioned herself behind the chalk line we'd drawn on the floor.

She then proceeded to put 51 cards straight into the hat. She threw them so quickly, and with such accuracy, that two of the cards collided in mid-air and one of them stayed on the brim. If it had not been for this fluke incident she would have achieved the maximum score of 52. As it was she had to make do with 51 and a half.

When she'd finished there was silence.

'It's a brilliant game!' she said, trying not to look as pleased with herself as she doubtless felt.

'Have you played before?' asked Harry quietly.

'Oh no,' said the woman. 'I didn't even know the game existed until today.'

None of us said a word.

'We'd better get a move on,' said the man, looking at his watch. 'We've got quite a walk ahead of us.'

They smiled, said goodbye and left.

A minute after they'd gone we were still sitting there in silence. Suddenly the door opened and the man put his head into the room. He was grinning.

'I didn't want to leave you too confused,' he said. 'I thought I should explain that my companion is a croupier in London.' He named a well-known casino. 'She deals cards for a living – spends her evenings dealing cards to Poker players. She can land a card on a sixpence from six feet away.'

And with that he was gone.

We sat in silence for several minutes.

'I suppose we should be grateful we didn't try to persuade her to put some money on the table,' said Thumper, breaking the silence.

Diggory Cholmondelay: Doing the Right Thing

There are all kinds of recognisable, easily defined family traits. Large noses run in some families. Some families specialise in receding chins. In other families the members are all very tall. Sometimes all the family members are very short. And in some families it is large, floppy ears which give the game away.

But the recognisable trait in the Cholmondelay family was eccentricity. By this I don't mean the sort of artificial, manufactured eccentricity which has become popular among individuals who are desperate to create for themselves a career on television, or in some branch of the entertainment business, but the sort of natural, unconscious eccentricity which was once so common among the British middle and upper classes; the sort of wild, unfettered eccentricity displayed by that great Victorian John 'Mad Jack' Mytton.

Diggory Cholmondelay's grandfather, Ambrose, was certainly eccentric.

As a relatively young man, Ambrose Cholmondelay had been a keen cricketer. Sadly, his enthusiasm far outweighed his talent and he had never been able to achieve the representative honours which he sought. Nevertheless, he did everything he could to tip the scales in favour of his playing for some sort of representative team.

In 1887, C Aubrey Smith (later to be knighted and to achieve eternal glory by playing stern patriarchs in Hollywood movies) captained a cricket team which visited Australia. Smith was a good player, a fast bowler, who had played for Cambridge University and Sussex and who later captained the England side in South Africa. When Cholmondelay was omitted from the players selected for Smith's tour he paid his own fare to Australia and, entirely at his own expense, followed the team around in the constant hope that injuries or illness might one day result in the captain inviting him to play. After six weeks, his dream was fulfilled. A broken leg, a bad case of the pox and a seven day prison sentence for punching a policeman meant that Smith lost three players and had only ten fit men when he needed eleven. Cholmondelay finally had his chance. In the first innings he scored three runs and in the second innings he scored nought. He didn't bowl in the match and he didn't play again on the tour. But he had achieved his ambition.

In their middle years Ambrose's wife, Fanny, achieved some notoriety of her own after cutting up a painting that experts had described as a masterpiece and valued at over £20,000 – a huge sum at the time.

The painting, by J.M.W.Turner had been titled 'Shipwreck in a Gale' and had been purchased by Ambrose's father. It hung above the mantelpiece in the dining room and Fanny hated it. She said it was horribly gloomy and made her feel depressed whenever she looked at it. Instead of simply moving the painting to another room, or selling it, she told two servants to take it down and remove it from the frame. She then cut the canvas into squares and had her personal maid make two cushions from it. They must have been the most valuable cushions ever made. It was an appropriate error of judgement for Fanny Cholmondelay herself admitted that her greatest claim to fame or admiration was that she always had well-plumped-up cushions in her home. 'You won't go into a room anywhere in this house and find a squashed cushion!' she once told an astonished Dr Brownlow.

In later life, Ambrose Cholmondelay's main hobby was rearranging the caskets in the family vault. Every Sunday evening he would go down into the vault, accompanied by the head gardener and a terrified pot boy and move the coffins around.

'Let's put the my great, great uncle Norbert Cholmondelay on the top shelf and move my grandmother over there by my great aunt Noreen Cholmondelay,' he would say, and the three men would then spend an hour or two lifting, pushing and pulling heavy, lead-lined coffins.

I gather that there never seemed to be any reason for any of this.

It was, according to Diggory, all done according to whim; it was like a huge three dimensional game of chess but without any plan or logical conclusion.

Even when he himself was mortally ill, the frail Ambrose insisted on being carried down into the vault so that he could supervise the final arranging of the caskets. Terrified that someone might come down and carry on the shuffling after he had chosen everyone's final resting place, he had the estate blacksmith come in and fix the coffins where he wanted them. The blacksmith put huge iron bands around the coffin and fixed them to the stone walls of the crypt with iron pegs. Naturally, Ambrose left the most prominent position vacant ready for his own coffin. And he made sure that there was no chance of his final resting place being moved. He left instructions that when his coffin had been placed in position it too should be fastened in place with thick iron bands.

Finally, two more things seemed to me to cement his reputation as an eccentric. First, it was Ambrose who devised a new family motto and had the words 'Nullum Crimen Neque Unguento Fugit Noster Escutcheon' ('no flies in our ointment, no blots on our escutcheon') carved on the stone arch above the driveway to the house and then repeated on the stone portico. Second, Ambrose, who was 102 when he died, always carried a walking stick made from a bull's penis (known in country areas of England as a pizzle stick). And he delighted in telling strangers the origins of his stick.

My predecessor, Dr Brownlow, told me that as a courtesy he called in to see Ambrose on the day of his 100th birthday but was told by the butler, that Mr Cholmondelay Senior was in London attending a celebration lunch. Dr Brownlow asked if he could call round to see him that evening, on his return, but was told that it would not be possible since Mr Cholmondelay had an appointment to play tennis with the vicar when he got back from London.

Ambrose's son, who was Diggory's father, was called Roderick, and he exhibited his eccentricity in an entirely different way. I met him only once or twice but he was unforgettable. He insisted on being addressed as 'General' though he had never served in any of the armed services. He would get very cross if people addressed him as anything else and in his later years he would simply ignore anyone who addressed him as 'Mister'.

Roderick and his wife both had flamboyant, well-groomed moustaches though hers was slightly more luxurious than his.

While the hair on her upper lip was growing well, the hair on the top of her head appeared to have pretty well abandoned the struggle to survive. The general's wife had responded to this not, as some women would have done, by spreading the remaining hair over the whole of her scalp, but by having her hair cut very short, militarily short. The result was that she had a head partly covered in the sort of steel grey bristle which was once popular with the more mature officers serving the Kaiser Wilhelm. If it had not been for the fact that she had given the general three children and had, in the luxury of the uppermost reaches of middle age, developed a bosom of such impressive proportions that she looked rather like one of those figureheads which used to be attached to the prows of sailing ships back in the days when ships had rigging and sailors had scurvy, I would have wondered what would have been found if a geneticist had taken a close look at her chromosomes.

The general also had a shortage of scalp hair and he disguised this by wearing a toupee; a rather threadbare hairpiece which, he once told me proudly, had originally belonged to his father and, before that, had adorned the balding pate of his father's older brother.

I don't know what colour the wig had been when it first saw the light of day, but it had been dyed many times and it had reacted badly to the various dyes and chemicals with which it had been assaulted, and by the end it had taken on a rather alarming hue; a sort of pearlescent henna with flecks of maroon scattered about. The 'General' seemed to feel that the significance of the heritage and antiquity of the hairpiece far outweighed its rather bizarre appearance. Indeed, I think he had been wearing the wig for so long that it no longer looked in the slightest bit odd to him. He kept it on his bedside table so that he never needed to be seen without it. It was not uncommon for him to put it on back to front and to wear it that way all day, blissfully unaware of the consequences and quite certain in his mind that the glances he received when out and about were entirely of recognition and admiration. ('Golly, there goes the General. Doesn't he look smart!' And not: 'Look at that old fool. He's got his wig on back to front.') The effect of eccentricity was enhanced by the fact that although he had shrunk considerably in his later years, he insisted on wearing the clothes he'd worn when he had been younger, despite the fact that they were several sizes too big for him. His shirt collar gaped so much around his neck that he looked rather like a friendly and inquisitive tortoise peering out of his shell.

The 'General' might have appeared to some to be a couple of sandwiches short of a good picnic but I always found him to be full of clever ideas.

'Always buy good hats and good shoes,' he once told me. 'They'll look better and last longer. In the long run they'll save you money and people will treat you with more respect.'

I once stood with him in the house when he was locking his back door. Most people in the village never locked their doors but the 'General' did so. He said it was necessary because he'd acquired a good many enemies in his life. He never explained who these might be. There were two locks on the door, both operated by huge, iron keys. He turned one key and closed one of the locks but left the other unlocked.

'Aren't you going to lock the other one?' I asked him.

He turned and looked at me, very sternly. 'If you have two locks on a door you should always leave one of them undone,' he told me. 'Then if someone tries to get in he will always be locking one of the locks and unlocking the other.'

Once he'd locked the door, he set a fierce looking man trap to catch anyone who did manage to get through his defences. He told me that he'd done this for at least thirty years and that his staff were always forbidden to leave their rooms after he'd locked up for the night. Since they undoubtedly knew about the man trap I doubt if he had any difficulty persuading them to obey this instruction.

The man trap, which had been specially designed to grip an intruder's leg without actually breaking it, was one of a number of items which the General had either invented himself or which he had taken an interest in developing or marketing.

He had, for example, taken a special interest in a machine to speed up eating which had been devised in 1879 by a French physician. The invention (which had been described as an 'electrical dining machine') was originally designed for a patient who could not swallow because of a paralysis but it was promoted as useful for those who wanted to get through meal times more speedily.

To use the machine the patient filled his mouth with food and then gave himself an electric shock in his jaws and throat. The food, it is said, then went down the oesophagus at the rate of 4,000 miles per second. (The General could not explain how the speed had been measured). It was reported that a man using the electrical dining

112

machine could consume an entire, exquisite French dinner, including all the season's delicacies, wine, coffee and dessert in one minute and fourteen seconds.

The General, who was a committed gourmand, had worked out that this machine could save him 1,200 hours a year – time which he could spend more fruitfully on his various enthusiasms. More significantly, he reckoned that the machine could reduce the amount of time his employees spent eating. The Cholmondelay family fortune rested upon the efforts of a factory in the West Midlands which made a variety of hinges for doors and windows and, after some work with a pencil and a large piece of paper, the General had concluded that productivity could be increased by 12% if all employees were instructed to consume their meals with the aid of the 'electrical dining machine'. Sadly, his aims were thwarted by the trade unions who (inexplicably and in his view unforgiveably) objected vehemently to the proposal.

As if all this wasn't enough to merit him being described as eccentric, the 'General' had insisted on filling the gardens of the family home with a number of statues. The really odd thing was that the statues were all identical. They consisted of a woman who was standing on a stone plinth, who had clearly lost her bath towel and appeared to be reaching out expecting someone to hand her another. The statue was based on the General's wife. I never counted the statues but the butler, a long-serving family retainer, assured me that there were over ninety of them spread around the grounds. Many of them were almost hidden and it could, I gather, be quite startling to see one of these statues suddenly coming into view from a position behind a tree. The butler told me that since the statues had been put into place, the amount of poaching had fallen considerably.

In a way, you could argue that all this history is irrelevant to Diggory, the patient with whom I am here concerned. But I don't think it is irrelevant because it helps to set the scene and, in a small way, explains and defines why he was the man he became. (To this I must add the rider that if we ever think we truly understand another human being, or how they were changed by life and circumstances, then we are almost certainly deluding ourselves.)

Young Diggory (as he was called, right until the day of his death) was an unusual man with massive eyebrows which looked like two tangled collections of those big spiders you often find in the darkest corner of the garage. He once told me that the only thing he considered important was to try to do the right thing. And I do think he always tried to do the right thing, though it is possible that doing the right thing as he saw it probably wasn't always necessarily what other people might have regarded as the right thing.

Diggory himself had his own mild eccentricities which had slowly developed through the years and which had blossomed when his father, the General, had died and he had inherited the house.

First, he was writing a history of the house where his family had lived since the 16th century. He had been working on it for seven years and had got as far as 1843. He reckoned he needed another 35 years to finish it. When he told me this he was 78-years-old. He gave me these details without any suggestion that he felt that there might be a chance he would not succeed in finishing the book. At the time he seemed to assume that if he needed another 35 years then God would give him another 35 years. And at the time it seemed by no means impossible for I don't think I'd ever known anyone in their 70s to be as determined to defy their age. He had a heart condition which had been diagnosed thirty years earlier but he still marched around the estate as though he were setting off on a route march and he could still do a full day's work in the gardens. I had warned him that he should take special care when the weather was really cold.

'Stay inside if it's freezing!' I warned him. 'Your heart will have to work extra hard when the weather is really cold. And you mustn't try working in the garden when it's very cold. In fact you shouldn't even go walking round the garden when the temperature is really low.'

Despite my warnings, I knew that all the year round, whatever the weather, he drove an open car, an old Bugatti which must have been worth a fortune but which he treated as just another, ordinary vehicle. He never wore an overcoat a hat or a scarf. Even if it was pouring down or snowing he would drive around without any protection against the elements. He always wore a version of the same suit, a three piece tweed creation which was so thick that it would doubtless keep him warm and cosy in a snow storm but which must have been unbearably hot in the summer. (He never wore the suit without the waistcoat.) He had a new suit delivered to him on the 1st of January each year. A tailor from Savile Row in London came to the house in November to take the measurements. When the new suit arrived, Diggory always burnt the old suit.

Thinking about Diggory's Bugatti reminded me that he once told me that he always put a chocolate into the car radiator every 1,000 miles. When I asked him why on earth he did this he told me that his father had done the same thing and had never had any trouble with the radiator.

'What sort of chocolate?' I asked him.

'Oh, I don't think it matters much as long as it's something with a soft centre. I wouldn't put in one of those toffee ones.'

I was tempted to try this in the radiator of the Rolls Royce which I had inherited from Dr Brownlow but I never managed to find the courage.

Diggory's only concession to his age was to wear a hearing aid. However, the hearing aid was, to say the least, a little unusual. Diggory had made it himself and it consisted of nothing more than a bit of plastic covered wire. One end of the wire was fixed into his ear with a small piece of rubber cut from an eraser and the other end was stuck into the top pocket of his jacket. 'Does it work?' I asked him one day. 'Of course it does,' he said. 'When strangers see it they naturally assume that I'm deaf and so they talk more loudly and more clearly.'

Oh, and one other thing: like his father, Diggory had an impressive collection of walking sticks. Like his ancestors, Diggory didn't do anything by halves. I suspect that he had the largest collection of walking sticks in Britain. Come to think of it, I suspect that it was probably the more comprehensive collection in Europe. He had a stick which he claimed a Zulu had cut out of a knobkerrie and had used at the Battle of Rorke's Drift; a stick which had been used by the Emperor Franz Joseph and a very fine ebony and silver stick which had been carried by the famous actor Sir Henry Irving. Altogether he had over 500 walking sticks. I used to tell him that if he ever injured a leg he'd be so spoilt for choice that by the time he'd decided which stick to use, he would have recovered. In the event, when he did sprain an ankle, and found that he needed a stick, he insisted on my providing him with a plain common or garden stick provided by the National Health Service. When he'd recovered, I had a devil of a job to persuade him to hand it back. He wanted to keep it for his collection.

Even without these fairly overt signs of eccentricity, Diggory would have qualified as a keeper of the family's sacred flame for his eating habits.

I didn't discover his dietary habits until I gave him a medical when he was 73-years-old. He needed the medical because he was taking out a mortgage to buy a farmhouse that was a couple of miles from his house. Every time any property remotely close to him came onto the market, he insisted on buying it. He was terrified of anyone infringing on his privacy. The company making the loan was insisting on a full medical because Diggory weighed slightly over 20 stones.

Now, I don't think it is an exaggeration to say that the English have always been fond of having a good time. Over the centuries, England has had plenty of gourmets, more than enough gourmands and, without a doubt, a good many old-fashioned gluttons.

Back in the 14th century, Edward III had made a valiant effort to get things under control. He laid down strict rules for eating and drinking. He ruled that commoners were forbidden to eat dainty dishes or consume costly drinks and he limited the main meal of the day to two courses with each course to consist of no more than three dishes. And he prohibited servants from eating fish or flesh more than once day.

Naturally, however, his son Lionel (known as the Duke of Clarence) wasn't affected by these silly rules and at his wedding feast there were no less than 30 courses. The leftovers fed 1,000 people. And his grandson, King Richard II, didn't take much notice of Edward either. For his Christmas dinner in 1399 the cooks butchered 28 oxen, 300 sheep and too many chickens to count. A total of 300 servants were needed to carry the food about.

From then on the rules were ignored – as long as you were rich enough to buy all the food you wanted to eat. Richard Neville, the Earl of Warwick, required six oxen to be killed every day for breakfast, though to be fair I don't suppose he ate them all himself.

In England, the royals, the aristocracy and the plain old stinking rich had always had big appetites. And they had invariably washed down their huge meals with fairly vast quantities of ale. The aim was always to have bread as fresh as possible but preferred to drink beer that had been brewed at least a year earlier. Both Henry VIII and

Elizabeth always started the day with a beef steak and a cup of ale for breakfast.

The Cholmondelays may not have been royal or aristocratic but they followed the aristocratic style when it came to eating.

'What did you have for breakfast?' I asked Diggory Cholmondelay at the beginning of my examination.

'A whole grapefruit, a haddock, sautéed chicken liver served in claret with mushrooms, kedgeree and fresh strawberries. I finished up with three toasted muffins served with fresh butter and black cherry jam.'

'And for lunch?'

'Well, before I got to lunch I had my elevenses.'

'And what did you have for your elevenses?'

'A bowl of lobster bisque and a selection of patisseries.'

'Right,' I said, making a note of all this.

And so it went on. He had his luncheon at 12.30 pm, at 2.30 he had coffee and cakes, at 4.00 he had afternoon tea consisting of scones, crumpets, sandwiches and a pot of tea and at 7.00 pm sharp he had an 8 course dinner. At 10.00 pm he had supper which always consisted of Welsh rarebit and cocoa.

It was not difficult to see why Diggory weighed considerably more than might be considered optimum for his five feet seven inches.

'And I have kickshaws constantly available between meals,' he told me.

'What is a kickshaw?'

'Oh, a little something foreign, fancy and rather insubstantial. The ones we have served here are always pastry parcels with something like a bit of chicken or some chopped dates inside. They're a bit like deep fried samosas. We have them stuffed with gooseberries, raspberries, shrimp, fresh tomato and mozzarella, salami and anchovy. The thing is that the kickshaw should always provide a gustatory surprise. You don't know what you're going to get until you bite into it. I'm surprised you've not heard of kickshaws, doctor. Dear old Samuel Johnson was a great kickshaw enthusiast.'

'Do you eat any vegetables?' I asked.

'Oh yes,' he told me quite proudly. 'I have a packet of cheese and onion crisps at least twice a day. So that's four vegetables isn't it?'

'Four?' I said, puzzled.

'Two helpings of potato and two helpings of onion,' he replied quite seriously.

I honestly didn't know what to say to that.

The other thing I remember about Diggory Cholmondelay was that his dog went to Peter Marshall's shop every morning to fetch his copy of *The Times*.

Peter had stopped delivering newspapers (he claimed it was never possible to break even on delivering papers) and so several people in the village had trained their dogs to go to Peter's shop to collect their daily papers. At one point there were three people who did this and occasionally the three dogs would arrive together and queue politely to be served. Diggory's dog was, however, the only one which was equipped with a special satchel strapped to his back. Diggory didn't like having his morning newspaper with a wet patch on it where it had been in the dog's mouth. Peter would put *The Times* into the satchel and if Diggory had any extra order, he would enclose a note asking for a packet of pipe tobacco, a box or matches, a magazine or whatever it was that he wanted. Peter would then put the requested items into the satchel along with the newspaper. I had thought about sending Ben along to fetch my papers but Miss Johnson, my receptionist, had to pass Peter's shop on her way to Bilbury Grange and so she'd always called in and collected our newspapers, fresh bread and milk.

Diggory was single until he reached his 78th birthday and half way through the year to his 79th birthday, he abandoned his bachelorhood and married Edna Beveridge, a woman who had been a maid in the Cholmondelay household since her 14th birthday and who had eventually risen through the ranks to become Diggory's housekeeper. She had worked for the family for over 60 years when she eventually accepted the final promotion available to her and became the chatelaine.

'It doesn't make much difference to me,' she told me a month after the wedding when I met her at the Cholmondelay's house.

I'd been called to attend an under gardener who'd stuck a fork in his foot. This was no rarity in Bilbury. At least twice a year I saw someone who had stuck a fork through a foot. Hector O'Malley, a retired railway engineer who had an extensive vegetable garden successfully speared his right foot an average of once a year for at least a decade.

'I've been Mr Diggory's mistress since two years after I arrived at the house and my work hasn't changed one jot over the years,' she told me. 'I still warm his bed and supervise the staff, same as I've always done. I still organise the meals and run the household. As far as I'm concerned nothing has changed. I emptied his bedpan before we were married and I still empty it now. I'm not having anyone else emptying his bedpan.'

'Do you still call him Mr Diggory?' I asked her, slightly surprised.

'Oh yes, of course I do. That's his name. What else am I going to call him? He's been Mr Diggory to me since I was a slip of a girl.'

Diggory Cholmondelay had been her life and, it turned out that she had been his life too.

Six months after the wedding, Edna came to see me.

'I think there's something wrong with me,' she reported.

I waited.

I knew her well enough to know that she would eventually get round to telling me what was troubling her but that I would not get there any quicker if I tried to hurry her by asking questions.

'It's very personal,' she began.

I nodded and waited.

'It's a problem down below.'

'Ah.'

'But not what you're thinking.'

'No.'

'The other.'

'Right.'

'Trouble with my waterworks.'

'Oh dear. I'm sorry to hear that.'

'It's painful to pass.'

'Water?'

'Exactly, doctor. I knew you'd understand.'

I waited.

The temptation to ask for more information was powerful. But I resisted. My first thought that Mrs Cholmondelay was perhaps suffering from honeymoon cystitis, though this seemed relatively unlikely given that the relevant activities could have hardly changed as a result of her marriage.

'It's very cloudy.'

'Oh.'

'And there seem to be little pieces of something floating in it.'

'Little pieces of something?'

'Yes. Quite definitely.'

She opened her handbag and took out half a bottle of Bell's whisky. But the bottle didn't contain whisky. It contained something that was obviously a urine sample but which looked more like soup. She handed the bottle to me. I put it down on my desk. This was clearly more than a mere urinary tract infection.

'And I can't hold it in as I used to be able to.'

'Incontinence?'

She shook her head. 'I've never been abroad. We were going to have a honeymoon in Paris but we didn't go. Mr Diggory decided he wouldn't like flying.'

'Have you been leaking?' I asked, realising that Mrs Cholmondelay must have misunderstood me.

'That's exactly it.' She nodded.

She also told me that she had been suffering from back pain and that she thought she had a temperature.

'I need to examine you,' I told her.

'Oh I don't think that will be necessary,' she said, slightly shocked.

I insisted that to make a diagnosis I needed to examine her.

'With my clothes off?'

'Some of them, at least,' I said.

And so with some reluctance she removed a few layers and climbed up onto my examination couch.

The examination didn't tell me very much other than that Mrs Cholmondelay had a slightly unexpected fever and very high blood pressure, but her next remark startled me and led me to an alarming diagnosis.

'I've had to increase my tablets but they don't seem to stop the pain,' she said.

'What tablets are you taking?' I asked her.

I knew I hadn't prescribed anything for her for years.

She reached into her handbag and pulled out a packet of painkillers. 'I never go anywhere without them,' she said.

I looked at the packet and my blood went cold. The tablets were phenacetin.

Now, back in the 1970s, phenacetin was still used as an enormously popular painkiller.

First introduced in the 1880s by the same German company which had first introduced aspirin tablets to the market, phenacetin had been popular for years. There was never much logic to its popularity but some people preferred it to aspirin. The one thing it had in common with aspirin was that it could be used to bring down a temperature. It was also cheap. Paracetamol was the third of the really popular and widely used over-the-counter painkillers. All three were made widely available because it was thought that they were perfectly safe. They did not have the addictive qualities of the opiate painkillers such as morphine and heroin and, back in the 19th century and early 20th century laudanum. (Laudanum had been widely available without a prescription since it was a major constituent of a whole range of inevitably popular and well-thought of patent medicines. It was not long ago that it was possible to buy cough syrup for children that contained a morphine derivative. It was very popular.).

By 1970, however, it had become known that the regular use of phenacetin could cause serious kidney damage – serious enough to result in death. Like a good many doctors I had stopped prescribing the stuff and I had always tried to dissuade patients from buying it if they needed an over-the-counter painkiller from the pharmacy. The symptoms and signs of poisoning caused by phenacetin damage creep up on you slowly. By the time you notice them it is too late to do anything.

'How long have you been taking these?' I asked.

I had decided I needed to intervene. I could no longer rely on Mrs Cholmondelay telling me her story.

'Oh, a long time. At least twenty years.'

'And how many do you take?' I heard myself asking.

'No more than sixteen a day. They're quite expensive.'

'Where do you get them from?'

'A pharmacy we use sends them over to me once a week. We have a delivery of medicines and toiletries every Friday.'

'Don't they ever ask why you order so much phenacetin?'

'Of course not! Why should they? It's nothing to do with them, is it?'

'Do they know how many phenacetin tablets you're taking?'

'They certainly don't. They mind their own business.'

'How often do you take sixteen a day?'

'Oh, every day. They stop me having pains.'

'What pains?'

'I don't know – any pains. I just know that if I take the tablets then I don't have any pains. People my age always get pains.'

'But you've been taking them for twenty years?'

'To ward off the pains I might have got if I hadn't taken them,' she said. 'And they worked! I didn't have any pains.'

I now suspected that Mrs Cholmondelay was in serious trouble.

Phenacetin can and does cause serious kidney disease. It can produce renal papillary necrosis and interstitial nephritis – both of which are pretty deadly disorders. The fact that Mrs Cholmondelay had acquired very high blood pressure and had the symptoms and signs with which she had presented, made me suspect that she already had very serious kidney disease.

'I need to get some tests done,' I told her. 'And to get the tests done I need you to go to the hospital in Barnstaple.' As I told her this I reached for the telephone.

'When?' she demanded, clearly unhappy.

'Today, straight away.'

'Oh, I can't go today. We're having a delivery of quails' eggs this afternoon. I have to be there to receive them. And the wine merchant is bringing this month's delivery. I can't possibly not be there when he arrives.'

'Someone else will have to deal with the quails' eggs and the wine,' I told her. 'You need to go to the hospital. I'll ring your husband and ask him to come here to take you over there straight away.'

Mrs Cholmondelay looked as if she were about to protest but I was already on the telephone. I rang the hospital first and spoke to one of the consultants. He agreed to see her in his out-patient department. I then rang Mr Cholmondelay and asked him to come and take his wife over to Barnstaple.

'What's wrong with her?' asked Mr Cholmondelay.

I told him that I wasn't yet sure but that I needed to get some tests done.

Three quarters of an hour later, Mr Cholmondelay turned up in his Bugatti to take his wife over to the hospital.

And three hours after that I had the telephone call I'd suspected I would get – but had, nonetheless, hoped I wouldn't.

'I'm afraid we're pretty sure that your Mrs Cholmondelay has end stage kidney disease,' said the consultant. 'We're keeping her in for some more tests. But it looks as if both her kidneys are pretty well destroyed. She tells me that she's been taking 16 phenacetin tablets a day for years.' He sounded rather angry and critical.

'Yes,' I said. 'That's what she told me.'

'You didn't prescribe them?'

'I certainly didn't!' I said, rather defensively.

'I'm pleased to hear it,' said the consultant, rather less gruffly now.

Mrs Cholmondelay lasted another three weeks.

She never came home from the hospital.

Diggory Cholmondelay was destroyed by her death.

I don't think I have ever seen anyone more clearly devastated by the loss of a partner. He was quite lost without her. Although they had married only recently they had been together for virtually the whole of their lives. They had certainly been together for all their adult lives. It must have been difficult for them both for many of those years. When Diggory Cholmondelay's father had been alive, the pair had for years tried to keep their relationship secret from him. I suspect that just about everyone else in the house knew about it but for several decades the General either didn't know or he pretended not to know. During the Second World War, Diggory Cholmondelay had served his country in London, working in the Ministry because he'd been considered too old for active service and had, in any case, failed a service medical because of his heart condition. When he had returned from London at the end of the War he'd insisted that Edna should move into his bedroom on a full-time basis and although his father had resisted this, his objections had been easy to dismiss since he himself had bedded several members of the female staff and was suspected to have had at least two illegitimate children as a result of productive liaisons with chamber-maids.

'I am simply too full of years and sadness,' Diggory Cholmondelay said to me. 'Can you put me down, please.'

At first I didn't realise that he was serious. But he was.

'I have absolutely nothing to live for,' he said. 'Edna and I were together so long that it is quite impossible for me to exist without her. I have no reason to be.'

'Your book,' I reminded him. 'You have to finish your history of the house. You need to live to finish that.'

He shrugged. 'She was the only one who would have cared,' he said. 'If I finish it who will I tell?' He wiped his eyes with his handkerchief. 'We used to share everything,' he said. 'And apart from that time during the War, we were never apart. She wanted to come to London with me but I wouldn't let her. I thought it too dangerous. I felt safer with her down here. But I've always shared things with her. If I found something special in a junk shop or at an auction I would want to rush home to show it to her. If she saw a bird in the garden doing something unusual she would tell me about it. If I found a good bit in a book I was reading then I would read it out to her. And she'd do the same for me.'

He really did want me to end his life.

'I can't do that,' I told him gently.

I offered him pills to help him over the next few days.

He didn't want anything.

I talked to him for hours. Or, rather, I listened to him talk about Edna and the things they'd done together. I'm not sure that it helped him. In fact, in a strange way, I think it may have made things worse for him.

'I can't,' I said again and again when he repeatedly asked me to give him something to end his life.

'Then if you can't do anything just tell me how to do it,' he pleaded.

'I can't do that either,' I said.

He nodded, got up and left the surgery without another word. I can still remember the way he walked away the last time I saw him in my surgery; head bowed, a broken human being.

It was winter when Edna died and it was one of the hardest winters we'd had for some years. There was deep snow everywhere and for a while the village was cut off from the rest of the world. The snow was so thick, and the roads so bad, that I couldn't get around in the Rolls Royce. I used one of Patsy's father's tractors instead. In most places the snow was three to four feet deep; in the hedgerows there were snowdrifts that were six feet deep. At Bilbury Grange we had Jack Frost patterns on the inside of our bedroom window and in the yard at the village school the children had made a slide that was over thirty feet long. The local television weather forecaster, sounding like a Victorian do-gooder had warned all old people to wrap up warm and to drink lots of hot soup. Two nights earlier, Thumper and I had blocked up the front door of the Duck and Puddle with a snow wall. The following day we realised that we'd sealed ourselves out of the pub and we had to spend an hour chipping away at what had turned into a wall of ice before we could get inside. Most of the wildlife was sheltering but I saw a redwing in the snow, puffed up, alert and searching for food. The redwings are unlike most birds in that they come to Britain for the winter. Most migrating birds travel in the other direction as autumn comes. Redwings come in search of the cold weather.

I'll never forget that bad winter.

I was driving round the village, checking on some of my older patients, and I was passing by the end of the driveway to Diggory's home one day when I saw a figure shovelling snow off the drive. It was about two months after Edna's death. It was snowing at the time and shovelling the snow seemed to me to be a rather pointless activity – like sweeping up leaves as the wind is blowing them from the trees. I could just make out the family motto 'Nullum Crimen Neque Unguento Fugit Noster Escutcheon' carved into the stone archway above him.

Whenever I saw it I couldn't help wondering how long it had taken skilled masons to carve that nonsense into the stone.

When I looked more closely I could see that it was Diggory doing the shovelling. To my astonishment he was naked to the waist and he was wearing old khaki knee length shorts. He appeared to be wearing a pair of ordinary shoes. I stopped the tractor, climbed down and waded through the snow to him. The snow was so deep that it came up higher than the tops of my Wellington boots. It didn't really matter because my trousers and socks were already soaking wet. I could see the clouds of mist created by his breath.

'What the devil are you doing?' I demanded. 'You'll catch your death of cold!'

Diggory just looked at me and nodded. He stuck his shovel into the snow and lifted up another pile of the stuff, tossing it carelessly to the side of the driveway.

I remembered then that he had a bad heart. And I remembered my warning to him. 'Don't do anything energetic in the cold weather,' I told him.

'You'll kill yourself!' I said.

He stopped again for a moment, looked at me and smiled. 'What are you going to do about it?' he asked.

And I didn't know what I was going to do about it.

I thought about grappling with him and trying to carry him up to the house. He guessed what I was thinking.

'I'm older than you but I'm strong and I'm determined,' he said. 'If you try to drag me up to the house I'll fight you and the minute you're gone I'll be out again.'

'I could have you taken to hospital,' I told him.

He shrugged. 'I've got lawyers,' he said. 'You'd never keep me locked in.'

'But...'I began.

'It's the best way,' said Diggory. 'It'll look natural. There will be no shame. It'll be put down as an accidental death.' He stared at me and then added: 'Unless you insist on speaking up.'

I turned, walked back to the tractor, climbed aboard and eventually finished my visits. Every few minutes I had stop to dry my eyes.

Diggory Cholmondelay died at 5.45 pm that afternoon. He was found in the snow by one of the gardeners who'd been sent to look for him. They called me straight away but when I got to the house he was dead. Since he had no children, the estate and all the family holdings went eventually to a distant relative who lived in Yorkshire.

I put 'heart attack' on the death certificate, which I wrote out myself.

There was no inquest. I decided that there was no need to trouble the police or the coroner.

And I still think I did the right thing.

Actually, I think that both Diggory and I did what we thought was the right thing to do.

Mr Forester's Bad Tempered Bowel

Although they lived little more than a quarter of a mile away from Bilbury Grange (in our part of the world that makes them close neighbours) I had seen very little of Sally and Algernon Forester.

They were, like most people in the village, rather quiet folk who preferred to keep 'themselves to themselves' as the saying goes. I don't mean to imply by this that they were unfriendly because they certainly weren't. If you passed by their house and they were in the garden they would wave and exchange a word or two about the weather. (If you made a list of the things that country folk discuss most commonly, the weather would always be at the top of the list. This was not because we didn't have anything else to discuss but because when you live in the middle of nowhere, and your village can get cut off overnight, the weather can have a huge impact on your life.)

If they heard that a neighbour was in trouble they would be there offering to help as soon as anyone in the village. So, for example, when Ollie Ruttle fell out of a tree in Barnstaple, broke his leg in three places and wasn't able to work, the Foresters were among the first to offer help. Ollie Ruttle was a self-employed gardener and one of his regular jobs was to cut the grass and keep the hedges tidy at the Foresters' place. The Foresters had a large garden and cutting, clipping and pruning took up two days a week. Mr Tuttle had only gone up the tree in order to try to rescue a kite for two small children, and he fell when a branch broke and deposited him unceremoniously on a patch of rock hard ground.

Legally, Mr Ruttle wasn't entitled to any sick pay and there was no doubt that he, his wife and their three children would have been in dire straits without outside help. Quite a few people took round parcels of food but, realising that you can't pay electricity and rates bills with apples and potatoes, Mr and Mrs Forester insisted on paying Ollie in full even though he wasn't able to do any work for them. Mrs Forester put two £10 notes into an envelope every week and popped the envelope through the Ruttle's letter box. It was a month before Mrs Ruttle saw who was delivering the envelopes.

Mr Forester was 74-years-old at the time. He was a large, imposing and elegant man who had impeccable manners and was invariably impeccably dressed. He always wore a jacket and a tie, whatever the weather, and could have been an ambassador to a small country, a head waiter or perhaps a judge. He had not, however, been any of those things. He had been an architect and a partner in a firm which had offices in the North of England but which had an international reputation. He had specialised in designing large buildings including, I believe, at least one opera house and a government building.

Whenever I talked to Mr Forester, I always thought he appeared a little distant, as though his body was present but his mind was somewhere else. And for a man who had earned his living designing buildings, he always seemed to me to be a bit disconnected from the world and remarkably unworldly. I had once stopped to talk to him and been astonished at how cut off he was from the world outside Bilbury. I don't think he could have told you the name of the current Prime Minister or answered any of those questions which doctors commonly ask when they are trying to decide whether or not an individual is suffering from dementia.

But Mr Forester was not in the slightest bit demented. He didn't really have the time to live in our modern world because he lived in the world of books: old books. He knew more about books, especially first editions, than anyone I've ever met.

His wife, Sally Forester, who was five years younger than her husband, was a sweet, diminutive lady who always dressed in the sort of long, down to the floor dresses once worn by Victorian ladies. She wore her hair, which was long and blonde, in ringlets, long, corkscrew shaped curls of a type usually only seen in those days in historical dramas shown in the cinema or on television, and she was the only woman I have ever seen carrying a parasol. She did this as though it were the most natural thing in the world to do. In fact, I believe she had at least three parasols. One was lemon coloured, one was light, dusky pink and one was white. They were all fringed and delicate, and Patsy said she thought they were the most beautiful things she'd ever seen.

Mrs Forester smoked cigarettes which she had especially made for her by a specialist tobacconist just off Jermyn Street in London. She smoked six of them every day. She never smoked more and she never smoked fewer. The cigarettes were made of a very smoky type of tobacco known as latakia and she smoked them through a six inch long holder made of jade and equipped, apparently, with a very early filtration system. The holder she used seemed extraordinarily long but she told me that it was exactly twelve inches in length and would be described by a tobacconist as being of 'theatre length'. (She told me that shorter holders are known as being of cocktail or dinner length but that it was apparently possible to purchase cigarette holders which were well over a foot long – these were apparently known as being of 'opera length' though I would have thought that if you went to the opera with a cigarette holder nearly two feet long there would be a risk that you would set fire to the hat or hair of the patron sitting in the row in front of you.) Mrs Forester explained that she used a holder because she hated having little bits of tobacco stuck to her lips and because it kept the smoke well out of her eyes. She also insisted that she was in good company since Jayne Mansfield, Audrey Hepburn, Rita Hayworth and Princess Margaret had all used cigarette holders.

Every time I talked to her I tried to persuade Mrs Forester to give up the smoking habit and every time we spoke about it she told me, with an engaging smile, that she understood that as a doctor it was my responsibility to admonish her for smoking but that she never believed anything that researchers or governments said and that she was quite certain that research would soon be published showing that smoking a modest amount of tobacco was good for your health. 'Moderation in all things,' she would say sweetly.

Alcohol was the only other drug either of them took. She had one glass of sherry every evening and he had one glass of whisky. Neither of them drank during the daytime. I do not think I am the first doctor to have noticed that many older people drink alcohol regularly but in very modest quantities. Indeed, most individuals who live to celebrate their 90th or even their 100th birthday say, with some pride, that they take a very small amount of alcohol every day. I sometimes wondered whether this modest, characteristic combination of self-indulgence and self-discipline might not be at least partly responsible for their longevity.

Not that the Foresters were particularly old. At the time of which I write he was just 74 and she was in her late sixties. They were a happy couple; contented and fulfilled. They had each other and while she looked after the garden, he collected books.

Collecting can become a mania, a mental illness in a way, and Mr Forester was well aware that his hobby had long since got out of control. Fortunately, he had clearly been successful in his profession and he could afford to indulge himself.

I have to say that in my experience it is by no means uncommon for a collector to spend more time and money on their obsession than they can really afford to spend.

A bookseller I knew once told me that one or two of his customers (they were nearly always men for it is, it seems, invariably men who become obsessive collectors) were so ashamed or embarrassed by their mania that they would go to extraordinary lengths to hide their new purchases. He said he had one customer who always asked for parcels of books to be sent to his club or sent to his home when he knew that his wife would be away. Another had piles of books parcelled up and sent to him labelled 'Rose Fertiliser'.

Over the years I had a number of patients who were keen collectors. For example, another patient of mine, whom I will call simply Paul, was an enthusiastic collector of rare coins. He spent far more on his collection than he could afford and he was extremely proud of the coins he had acquired. I remember he once came into my surgery with a small, wooden box containing an extraordinary collection of silver coins from the days of Queen Elizabeth I. He had bought them from a dealer in London. He asked me to take the box and to then sell it to him for £5, giving him a note of ownership which he could show to his wife. He had clearly paid far more than that, and far more than he could afford. I told him that since his wife was also a patient of mine I could not possibly take part in such a deception, but in truth I would not have taken part in it even if she hadn't been one of my patients. I think Paul managed to persuade Peter Marshall to agree to take part in the deception.

Over the years I learned so much from my patients.

I don't think doctors working in towns and cities ever had the time to spare to listen to their patients. The urban physicians

131

undoubtedly earned far more money than country doctors but I thought then, and still think now, that those of us who worked in the remoter parts of the country were richer in the real sense of the word.

I digress.

My apologies.

Let's get back to the Foresters.

They were, as a couple, like two halves of a pair of scissors, to use a phrase coined by Benjamin Franklin. They'd been married for the best part of half a century and they had, over the years, grown ever closer to each other.

The Forester's home, a beautiful Georgian house which they had lovingly restored, was full of books. I don't think there was a room other than the kitchen (and I suppose the bathrooms) that didn't have floor to ceiling bookcases on at least one of the walls and although he had a library of over 20,000 books, Mr Forester knew where every single book was positioned. He looked after them all as though they were rare orchids and once told me that he had, for a while, considered keeping his books upside down so that their upper spines would not be damaged when they were removed from their shelves. Fortunately, he decided against this and avoided any risk of damage by making sure that his books were stored fairly loosely on the shelves and weren't crammed in tightly.

Both the Foresters enjoyed good health and I did not often see them in the surgery.

Mrs Forester had some mild varicose veins for which I prescribed elastic stockings. These were not to cover the veins, since her long dresses did that very adequately, but merely to prevent the ankle swelling which can accompany swollen and inadequate venous drainage.

Mr Forester had once had a sore throat and he'd been to see me with an attack of indigestion which had come on after Christmas and had continued to annoy him well into January. The symptoms had disappeared after treatment with an antacid and had not returned. He had also suffered from irritable bowel syndrome for many years and the symptoms of this, bloating, a painful abdomen and occasional diarrhoea, had been with him for over three decades. He knew that both diet and stress could make his symptoms worse. If he ate too much fat or too much fibre then the symptoms would get worse but they would also worsen if he found himself in a stressful situation for any reason.

So, when Mr Forester came into the surgery I had no idea what his complaint might be. If I'd had to guess I would have guessed that he was having trouble with his irritable bowel syndrome again. IBS (which was in the 1970s still sometimes called by its original names of 'spastic colon' or 'mucous colitis') had for years been one of the most underestimated diseases there is. The pain caused by a bowel in spasm can be excruciating. And why shouldn't it be? It is well known that pain which is caused by muscle spasm is often the worst sort of pain. The pains caused by gall stones, kidney stones and child labour are all caused by muscle spasms. So why shouldn't the spasm of the huge muscles of the bowel be taken more seriously? It had long seemed to me that the medical profession (and the pharmaceutical industry) had more or less abandoned millions of patients simply because they underestimated a problem which they couldn't properly understand and couldn't think of a way to treat successfully.

Doctors, relying on what they had been taught, supplemented by what they had read in medical journals and medical textbooks, still believed that IBS was best treated with a diet heavy in roughage. To be honest, I had always felt that this was like trying to treat diabetes mellitus by telling patients to eat more sugar. I knew that it was often roughage that caused irritable bowel syndrome and that encouraging patients to take more roughage was more likely to exacerbate the problem than to cure it.

The professions didn't take IBS very seriously because there was no effective pharmacological remedy available. The healing professions were, I am afraid to say, dominated by the needs of the pharmaceutical industry and modern medical care was dominated by, and run for, interventionists in general and drug companies in particular. As a result, doctors could be hidebound and worryingly unimaginative. And, because IBS was neither a dramatic disease, nor a fashionable one, nor one that usually killed sufferers, the majority of doctors remained blisteringly ignorant about it. It was, I am afraid, a disease that was more likely to result in sniggers than sympathy.

Back in the 1970s, I had lost count of the number of patients who had told me that their doctor has told them that their symptoms could not be caused by IBS because 'the tests had come back negative'.

That was clever of them because I knew of no comprehensive and truly effective tests for IBS. The diagnosis had to be made on the basis of the symptoms and signs.

All this was all the more remarkable when you realised that IBS was one of the commonest of all chronic disorders. It was, for example, just as common as all the forms of arthritis put together and much commoner than many well-known and highly investigated diseases.

After the usual pleasantries, Mr Forester explained that he had recently suffered from a rather alarming series of what he called 'palpitations'. It seemed that it wasn't his IBS which had brought him to the surgery.

'It started two days ago,' he said. 'I had been pottering in the garden, not doing anything very strenuous, and I came indoors to sit in the conservatory for a while before dinner. Suddenly, I felt rather strange. I don't know how to explain it really but I felt weak and dizzy and it was rather alarming. I checked my pulse, which I do from time to time as a routine, just to check that my heart is beating and that I'm still alive, and I found that it was going so fast that I couldn't even begin to count it.'

'Do you know if your pulse was regular?' I asked him.

'I don't think it was,' he said. 'It seemed to be all over the place. There didn't seem to be any rhythm to it at all. I was so alarmed that I checked my blood pressure with a machine we have. An American friend bought it for me and sent it over. According to the machine my pulse was 156 and upwards and my blood pressure alternated between absurdly high and absurdly low. The machine lit up with all the little warning lights with which it is fitted.'

'Did you have any nausea?'

'No, no, nothing like that.'

'Were you sweating?'

'No, I wasn't really sweating. I got a bit nervous for a while and that made me sweat a bit. But I wasn't dripping with sweat. I've seen people sweat with heart trouble and I had nothing like that. I wasn't clammy for example.'

'But you didn't call me!' I said. 'Why on earth didn't you ring me? I could have been with you in five minutes!'

'I don't really know,' he admitted. 'After the initial shock I started to get used to the fact that my heart was all over the place and since I didn't have any pain in my chest or my arm or my jaw I didn't think I was having a heart attack.'

'You can have a heart attack without any real pain,' I pointed out.

'Yes, I had heard that,' he said. 'But to be honest I just wanted to sit and rest.' He took a big breath and paused before continuing. He seemed to have difficulty in taking in air. 'Actually,' he went on, 'there was another reason for not calling you.'

He seemed embarrassed but I urged him to continue and to explain what he meant.

'I was worried that if I turned up as an emergency you might think I needed to go to hospital. And I worried that if you sent me into hospital I would probably find myself being treated for heart disease. I've got several friends with heart disease and I know the regime. They're all taking drugs to control their heart beat and they're also all taking warfarin to stop their blood clotting.'

I nodded. 'But?'

'I know that there can be big problems with those drugs,' he said. He held up a hand. 'Before you tell me that they can save lives, I do know that. And I understand that people with serious heart trouble need to take drugs to keep them alive. But everyone I know who takes digoxin and warfarin has some problems with them. Their heart rate never seems to be normal and once you start on these drugs it seems impossible ever to stop them. And making sure that they aren't taking too much warfarin can be difficult.' He thought for a moment. 'There was something else that occurred to me,' he said. He struggled to remember. 'I should have written down all the things I wanted to say.' I waited for a moment or two. 'Oh yes,' he continued. 'I was also worried that I might end up being taken in for an angiogram. You know, that test where they stick needles into you and put tubes into your heart and then do tests and take pictures. I understand that can be a pretty risky procedure.'

'It can,' I agreed. 'I understand your fears. So, that's why you didn't want to go to the hospital? You didn't want to end up taking drugs to control your heart rate or being over-investigated. Is that right?'

'Well, yes, in a way, but also, no,' he said. He paused and swallowed. 'I'm finding this difficult to explain but I'm trying to be honest.'

'OK,' I said. 'Take your time.'

135

'The thing is,' he said, 'that I didn't think that my irregular heart beat was due to a problem with my heart. I know that sounds crazy but I've always been pretty in tune with my body and I didn't think my heart was failing me. You might think that I just didn't want to accept what was happening but that was very much how I felt at the time.'

'So, what did you think was causing the problem with your heart – if your heart itself was fine?'

'I had an enormous amount of wind that day,' he said. 'I want to talk to you about that, and to try to find out why, but for whatever reason I had massive amounts of wind in my abdomen. And the wind was pressing up on my diaphragm. I could feel it!'

I was beginning to understand what he meant. And I was also beginning to think that he might have been right not to want to go hospital. He had been absolutely right in his assumption that I might well have sent him to hospital. And he was certainly right in guessing that if he had been to hospital he would have been treated with an anti-arrhythmic drug such as digoxin and probably also an anti-coagulant such as warfarin.

'So, tell me what happened? You were sitting in the conservatory and your heart rate was all over the place and your blood pressure was going up and down like a yoyo. What happened next?'

'I just sat there for ages,' said Mr Forester. 'I had awful wind. I don't like to be vulgar but I couldn't stop burping. I felt that the only way that I could get relief from the discomfort I felt was to bring up the air in my stomach. I felt as though the air in my stomach was pushing up my diaphragm and, you'll probably think I'm mad, compressing my heart.'

'So you thought that maybe the wind was causing your palpitations, fibrillations, whatever they were?'

'Yes. Actually, what's the difference between palpitations and fibrillations? I've never understood that.'

'When you have palpitations you notice an irregular and rapid heart rate. It's sometimes said that palpitations are just fast and regular but that isn't really the case. Palpitations can be irregular. They can be caused by a problem with the heart itself but they can also be caused by agitation, by too much exercise or even by stress. Actually you can get palpitations from something you've drunk or eaten. For example, coffee is a common cause of palpitations. Most people will get palpitations if they drink enough strong coffee.'

'And fibrillations?'

'That's when the heart is quivering. The contractions are uncoordinated and rapid and irregular. There are two sorts of fibrillation: atrial fibrillation which involves the heart's upper chambers or atria, and ventricular fibrillation which involves the ventricles.'

Mr Forester frowned. 'It doesn't sound as if there's all that much difference.'

'There isn't. The difference is in the cause rather than what you feel. A fibrillating heart is usually beating fast and irregular but you can have palpitations that are fast and irregular. The main difference, I suppose, is that fibrillations usually signify some more fundamental problem. Palpitations can be serious but they can also be caused by something that isn't as serious.'

'I see.'

'Did you know that there is a theory in medicine that wind can be caused by heart problems?' I asked him.

'I didn't,' said Mr Forester. 'Do you believe that?'

I smiled. 'No, I don't really. I know that in medicine, just about anything is possible. But I don't think that heart disease is a direct cause of massive amounts of wind – the sort of quantities of wind that you can get with IBS – though I do suspect that heart disease may cause some burping. However, I do think that things can happen the other way round and that massive amounts of wind can be an apparent cause of heart problems.'

'Such as palpitations?'

'Such as palpitations.'

'So, you think I might have been right in assuming that the enormous amount of wind which I had was pressing on my heart?'

'Ah. No, not really. I don't think that the wind was pressing directly on your heart. But I do think it was possible that the wind was pressing on your vagus nerve.'

'What the devil is the vagus nerve?'

'The stomach and the heart share a common nerve supply – through something called the vagus nerve. Technically, the vagus nerve is also known as the tenth of the twelve cranial nerves.

'And if the wind pressed on the vagus nerve, it could cause palpitations?'

'That's my theory,' I told him. 'The trouble with the medical profession is that it is sometimes over-influenced by whether or not a treatment is available. If palpitations are caused by a heart problem, then those palpitations can be treated with wonderful, expensive drugs or by even more expensive, and profitable, surgery. But if the palpitations are caused by wind pressing on the vagus nerve then there isn't anything that doctors can do about it.'

'So, doctors prefer to assume that all palpitations are caused by heart disorders?'

'I suspect so. But remember this is just my theory. The medical establishment wouldn't agree with me and many doctors would think I'm being a heretic even to suggest it. New ideas and new ways of looking at things have never gone down well with the establishment. Doctors and nurses are dedicated to the interventionist philosophy. Doing something is their default. And most patients are eager to accept whatever treatments are offered.'

'So you don't think I was mad not to ring you? Sally was desperately keen to ring you and get you to come racing round.'

'How have you been since that bad attack of palpitations?' I said, unashamedly avoiding the question.

'I felt a bit weak for a few hours the next day but gradually I started to feel better. It took about six hours for the fibrillations to slow and for my heart to start beating normally again and afterwards I was exhausted. Oh and I yawned a lot too.'

'The vagus nerve also triggers yawning,' I told him.

I felt as though my diagnosis was coming together at last. 'If something is pressing on your vagus nerve then you'll probably start yawning. However, to the orthodox professional, yawning is just another sign that a patient is having a heart attack. Actually, just to make things even stranger, the vagus nerve can also cause pains in the left arm –mimicking a heart attack.'

'Gee,' said Mr Forester. 'I wonder how many people are being treated for heart disease when their real problem is wind caused by their irritable bowel syndrome?'

'I have no idea,' I admitted. 'Absolutely no idea.'

'And how many people have died because they were given drugs such as digoxin or warfarin which they didn't really need but which can kill people occasionally?'

'Again, I have no idea.'

'I am right in thinking those drugs can kill?'

'You are, I'm afraid. They can and do save lives but they can be lethal. For example, if the doctors or nurses get the dosage of warfarin wrong then a patient can have a bleed – resulting in a deadly stroke. And the whole problem gets worse because the drugs commonly used to treat an irregular heartbeat can also cause an irregular heartbeat.'

'So, a patient who has palpitations may be given a drug which causes more palpitations and so the doctors increase the dosage of the drug without realising that the drug they are giving is causing the problem?'

'I'm afraid so,' I said.

'Hmmm,' said Mr Forester, not entirely unreasonably.

I didn't say this to Mr Forester, but even then, back in the 1970s, I was beginning to realise that the older I got, and the more I knew, the more I had begun to realise that medicine really was still in the dark ages. We have to remember, I suppose, that it wasn't all that long ago that doctors claimed that smoking was good for the lungs, that cutting out long lengths of the intestine was a great way to cure all sorts of health problems and that deliberate blood-letting was a wonderful cure for many of the things that couldn't be cured by chopping out a dozen feet of bowel.

Generally speaking, doctors find it next to impossible to do nothing. This is partly because if they do nothing that rather suggests that they know nothing and partly because the best, easiest and quickest way to end a consultation is to hand over a prescription for something. Doctors also have a terrible (and frequently fatal) tendency to treat symptoms, or consequences, rather than causes.

'I've noticed something else recently,' continued Mr Forester. 'If I have a lot of wind then I find I have to get up at night to go to the loo. I thought it was my prostate gland at first. But do you think the wind could be responsible for my having to get up at night?'

I told him I thought it was about time I gave him a thorough examination. Having checked with my receptionist, Miss Johnson, that there were no more patients sitting in the waiting room, I told him to undress, and to lie down on my examination couch. I then gave him the full ten guinea examination (as my predecessor and mentor Dr Brownlow used to call it when he gave a patient as thorough and as exhaustive an examination as he could).

I even told Mr Forester to lie on his side, pull his underpants down and pull his knees up so that I could check out the size, shape and feel of his prostate gland.

At the end of half an hour, I told Mr Forester that I could find absolutely nothing wrong with him apart from some wax in his left ear, a long-standing case of athlete's foot, a very early cataract in his right eye and some small and insignificant varicose veins in both legs. His systolic blood pressure reading was raised slightly but his diastolic, the lower figure, was perfectly normal. His heart was perfectly regular and I could find no sign of any abnormality.

'You're in tip top condition for a man of 50,' I told him, when he was dressed and sitting again. I never liked to talk to patients about my findings while they were getting dressed.

'I'm 74!' he reminded me quickly.

I often found that patients who were over 70 were proud of their age. A child will tell you their age in an instant. And so will someone of retirement age.

'I know you are. But you're in tip top condition for a man of 50. It was a compliment.'

He smiled. 'Oh. Thank you! What about my prostate gland?' he asked. 'I take it that it was my prostate gland you were checking when you put the rubber glove on?'

'Your prostate is absolutely fine,' I told him. 'It isn't enlarged and it isn't hard or misshapen.'

'So it isn't because of my prostate that I've had to get up at night to pass urine?'

I shook my head. 'No, it isn't because of your prostate.'

'And it does only happen when I've got a lot of wind.'

'So I think we can safely assume that it's the wind in your bowel pressing on your bladder that makes you get up and go to the loo.'

'Crumbs. This damned IBS gets everywhere, doesn't it?'

I agreed with him. 'In my experience, IBS can cause a whole range of symptoms, including tiredness, muscle aches, an inability to concentrate and gastritis – to name just a few. In your case I think

140

your IBS has caused your heart problems and your bladder problems.'

'You definitely think that it was my IBS which triggered all those heart problems?'

I nodded. 'I do.'

'It's a bugger of a disease,' said Mr Forester. He sighed. 'Still, I should be grateful I suppose. I could have something far worse wrong with me.' He stopped for a moment. 'Do you ever think that maybe there is an angel up there who makes all the life and death decisions? Maybe tossing a coin to decide who has a heart attack, who falls off their bike and breaks a leg or who develops irritable bowel syndrome?'

I didn't know what to say to that. I hadn't actually thought of angels handing out diseases, like Father Christmas handing out presents at a children's party.

'Do you doctors have any idea what the devil causes irritable bowel syndrome?' asked Mr Forester. 'Haven't any of those bright research blokes worked it out yet?'

'I'm afraid no one has yet worked out what causes IBS,' I told him. 'There are all sorts of theories but there's still no real evidence to show precisely why the bowel can misbehave so badly. There are a few researchers trying to find solutions but from what I've seen I doubt if anything that helps us is going to be published before the 1980s at the earliest. By the early part of the 21st century I have no doubt that there will be a good many new theories, some hard evidence and some real remedies available. I have a suspicion that some of the alternative medicine therapies being put forward might work. And I know people are looking at the complex relationship between bacteria and IBS and there is even a theory that there is a possibility that fungal infections might interfere with the bacteria living in the bowel. However, we're still living in the 1970s and for the time being we have to go with what we've got!'

'Trust me to get a disease which no one understands!'

'Sadly, there are still a lot of things doctors don't understand,' I confessed. 'As a profession, doctors always like to pretend that they know more than they do! I think the theory is that if the doctor is confident then the placebo effect will work well and there will be a better chance of the patient recovering.'

'I understand that,' agreed Mr Forester. 'But sometimes it helps to know the truth rather than to be deceived with a load of waffle!'

'What you and I need to do now,' I said, 'is to try to work out together why your IBS has suddenly flared up and has been affecting you so badly. If we can find out what's triggered this recent trouble then hopefully we can stop it happening again.'

I always found it wise to try to work with a patient when dealing with a chronic disorder – particularly one which was a bit of a puzzle. Traditionally, most doctors preferred to do things 'to' their patients. Rightly or wrongly I preferred to do things 'with' them. I suspected that many doctors in the medical establishment would disapprove of my approach.

'Well, I've been very careful with my diet,' said Mr Forester. 'After all the years I've had it, I know which foods make my IBS worse and I've carefully avoided those. I know that I can't eat lots of fatty food, that I can't eat lots of food with roughage in it and that I can't eat too many sweet dishes – so I've been careful with all of those. I drink loads of fluids because I've found that my symptoms are worse if I'm a bit dehydrated. I've tried all the medicines you can buy over the counter and none of them has made the slightest difference.'

I was reminded, yet again, that human beings can get used to almost any chronic health condition; adjusting their lifestyle in some appropriate way and then just getting on with their life as best they can.

'So, the chances are high that your current problem must have been caused by something other than diet.'

'I agree. But why has it affected my heart and my bladder for the first time? Usually my IBS causes muscle cramps and quite a lot of pain but the pain is usually down here,' he said, rubbing his lower abdomen.

'Your problems have been worse because there's been more air in your bowel than ever before,' I explained. 'And the symptoms have changed because there is so much more wind.'

I explained that the pain that is so typical of irritable bowel syndrome appears to be caused directly by wind inside the bowel.

'Normally, the muscles of the bowel wall move food along the intestine by compressing and squeezing and pushing it. It's a process called peristalsis. My theory is that when there is a lot of wind inside the intestines, the bowel wall is stretched with the result that the bowel automatically contracts in an attempt to move along the food that it mistakenly believes is there. But there isn't any food there, just wind, and so the bowel keeps contracting and relaxing and then goes into spasm.'

'So if my diet hasn't changed, and I have been avoiding all the specific foods which I know can make my IBS worse, what the devil has changed?'

'There is one other huge factor that we've ignored so far,' I told him. 'Stress.'

'Oh, I don't think that could be my problem,' said Mr Forester. 'I've been retired for a few years now. I don't commute, I don't have clients to worry about, I don't have to rush around the world to check on projects. I just live a quiet life, at home with my wife, my books and the garden.'

I knew by the way he told me this that there was something he wasn't telling me; some significant problem that he was either not acknowledging or that he didn't want to tell me about. I didn't say anything, but just waited.

I knew that remaining silent was often the quickest way to obtain information. Witnesses in court, interviewees on television, job applicants and patients in a surgery or a clinic will invariably reveal more, and often divulge information which they might otherwise have kept to themselves, if they are allowed to think during a period of silence. In those circumstances most people feel uncomfortable if a silence goes on too long. They feel a need to fill the empty space and unless they are extremely imaginative, and good liars, they will, more often or not fill the gap with truths which have been suppressed or hidden or just forgotten.

So I just looked at Mr Forester and waited. It seemed as if the silence lasted an hour or so. Actually, it lasted less than half a minute.

'There is one thing that has been worrying me a little,' he said at last.

Again I said nothing and waited. I just nodded, hoping that it would appear to be a nod of encouragement.

'There is something that has been on my mind.'

I still said nothing. Even then I knew that if you spoke too soon when someone was about to reveal something they'd previously

143

tried to hide then you could spoil the moment. So I just sat and looked at him and waited.

Mr Forester sighed.

'I have a brother,' he said. 'Or, rather, I had a brother.'

'I didn't know that,' I said.

'His name was Simon and he was two years younger than me.'

'You speak of him in the past tense.'

'Yes. He died.'

'When was that?'

'About two weeks ago. I had a letter from a solicitor.'

'I'm sorry to hear that.'

'He wasn't a good man,' said Mr Forester. 'In fact he was pretty much a bad egg I'm afraid. He went to prison once or twice.'

And slowly, with considerable difficulty, Mr Forester told me the story of his brother. He hadn't seen him or spoken to him for over a half a century. The brother had been expelled from school at the age of 16 for running some sort of primitive protection racket. Mr Forester's parents had found him a job with a shipping company but after six months he lost that job because he was caught stealing. And on and on it went. He was given chance after chance but he always managed to mess things up. He always promised to make an effort but he never quite managed to 'do the right thing', as Mr Forester put it. At the age of 19 he was sent to prison for theft. And in prison he'd killed a man with a home-made knife.

'The family pretty much disowned him when he was sent to prison,' said Mr Forester. 'I always felt guilty about it but there wasn't anything I could do. When he came out of prison he contacted me at my office and I sent him money. He didn't want to meet me and I didn't want to meet him. He just asked for money. So I sent him what I could afford. Actually, I sent him more than I could afford. And that went on for years. I would forget about him and then I'd suddenly get a scribbled note demanding money. He always gave a Poste Restante address somewhere. Occasionally it was in London. Sometimes it was in the Far East. I don't know what he was doing but I think it had something to do with drugs. He bought a boat and I think he was using it to smuggle drugs. I know he bought a boat because I paid for it. He didn't want to see me any more than I wanted to see him. Several times he threatened that if I didn't send him money he would find some way to embarrass me. He always demanded cash. I had to go to the bank, parcel it up and post it off to whatever address he was using. He obviously knew what I did for a living and he said he'd turn up at the opening of a building I had designed or come to my offices; he threatened to stand in the lobby and tell the clients that I wasn't properly qualified or that I was a thief or a drug dealer or whatever came to his mind. What sort of person does that?'

'Why didn't you tell the police? Call his bluff?'

'I couldn't do that because I was frightened of him. He'd always been dangerously unpredictable. I was worried what he might do. And there was something else.'

He looked down at his hands and grimaced. He then caressed his lower abdomen. I guessed that he was having an intestinal spasm. I now knew why his IBS had got worse so suddenly. It had nothing to do with what he was or was not eating.

'What was the something else?'

'Sally didn't know he existed. I'd never told her about him. I don't know why. Well, yes, I suppose I do. I was ashamed of him as well as frightened of him – and of what he might do.'

'Does she still not know about him?'

He shook his head. 'I never wanted her to know about him. I wanted to protect her. I am, was, ashamed of him and everything he did with his life, but it was more than that. I never wanted him in our life in any real way. I always felt he would, I don't know, just dirty things. Do you understand?'

'I think so. Yes, I think I do. So, what did the solicitor want?'

'He'd traced me as the sole relative. It can't have been difficult. I'm not difficult to find. He said there was no one else to pay the funeral costs. And there were some small debts. Not much, nothing I can't easily manage.'

'So, what's the problem? Can't you just send the solicitor a cheque?'

'Yes, of course. I can do that. And I don't feel I need to go to his funeral. I loathed my brother and he wasn't part of my life.'

'But Sally doesn't know? Does she have to know?'

'When I stopped working I closed my business account. Sally and I only have a joint account. And Sally does our accounts.'

'So, she would wonder why you were sending a cheque to a solicitor she'd never heard of?'

'Exactly.'

'I understand. That's something of a dilemma.'

'The worry of it has been making me feel quite ill.'

'It's also the cause of the problem with your IBS.'

'Do you think so?'

'Definitely.'

'I suppose I must have known that his day would arrive eventually,' said Mr Forester. 'And I'm glad that he died first. I wouldn't want him to have approached Sally after I'd gone. That would have been awful.' He swallowed hard. He seemed to be having difficulty in getting his breath.

'Are you OK?' I asked him.

He nodded. 'I can feel my bowel griping,' he said. 'And the wind feels as though it's pushing up on my diaphragm again. I didn't mention that before but I could feel it pushing up.'

'You have to tell Sally,' I told him. 'You have to explain everything to her today. You have to tell her that you have a brother you've never mentioned and you have to tell her why you never mentioned him. You have to tell her about the demands for money and you have to tell her about the solicitor's letter and this last request for money.'

'Do you think so?'

'Definitely. My predecessor, Dr Brownlow, once said that worry is interest on a debt that needs to be paid. Until you've dealt with this, and brought the secret out into the open, then you'll be worrying. Besides, you don't have much choice. You need to send a cheque to the solicitor and to do that you have to tell Sally.'

'How the devil do I do that?'

'Just tell her. She'll understand. And then it will all be over. And I can pretty well guarantee that your IBS will go back to being an annoyance instead of the terrible burden that it has become. You are anxious now not because of your brother – he's gone and cannot hurt you again – but because of the secret. And as secrets go it's not a particular potent or toxic one.'

Mr Forester stood up. 'You're right!' he said firmly. 'And if I'm going to do it then I need to do it now.'

He shook my hand and left.

Three hours later he telephoned me.

'Sally knew about him,' he said. 'She said my mother told her all about him. She never said anything to me because she thought it would upset me to talk about him. But she knew all about him. She's written the cheque to the solicitor.'

'Do you feel any better?'

Mr Forester laughed. 'Better?' he said. 'I feel as if a ten ton weight has been taken off my head. For the first time in a fortnight I feel alive.'

He promised to call me if the palpitations ever came back.

But I didn't hear from him for six months. And then he just came in because he needed the wax syringing from his left ear. I'd forgotten to do it before.

I am not saying that my theories were correct, of course. You can't draw conclusions from a single case. But Mr Forester had no more palpitations and didn't have to get up at night to pee.

Well, not for five years anyway, and then it was a completely different story.

The Christmas Eve Surgery

Christmas was always a special time for Patsy and me at Bilbury Grange. We enjoyed the usual trappings – including stockings hanging from the mantelpiece, candles on the dining table, a huge yule log ready to slide into the hearth so that it would provide heat for the whole day, a bowl of nuts and, of course, a beautifully decorated Christmas tree.

We didn't like to have a live tree in the house, not because they tend to drop their needles on the carpet but because they invariably die afterwards. Even if you have a tree which still has its roots, and you keep it well watered, the chances are high that it will die when you have transplanted it into the garden. So, rather than a live tree, we had a large, artificial tree which we had purchased from Peter Marshall. It cost us £5 and just fitted into our drawing room. We always decorated it with Victorian baubles and coloured fairy lights.

It is often said that the idea of having a Christmas tree brought indoors and decorated with candles and other finery was introduced into England by Prince Albert but strictly speaking this isn't true. Prince Albert didn't so much introduce the habit of having a Christmas tree as reintroduce it back into the country where the idea had originated.

Having a tree in the house had been a common custom in England for many centuries before the miserable, humourless Puritans purged Christmas of all the jollity, frivolity and exuberance.

The really odd thing is that it was an English missionary called Boniface who introduced the Christmas tree to Germany back in the 8th century. Saint Boniface, to give him his proper honorific, was originally called Wynfrith and started out his religious life as a Benedictine monk. Then, when he became a priest, Pope Gregory sent him to Germany with papal orders to convert the heathens living east of the Rhine. After he'd taken time out to introduce the Christmas tree into his adopted land, poor old Boniface was killed by a band of Frisians (islanders from the Frisian isles rather than misspelt black and white cows from Friesland) while he was reading the Bible to a bunch of recent converts. Feeling pretty bad about things, the authorities tried to make up for the unhappy ending by making him a saint.

The other odd thing is that at the time when we gave the Christmas tree to the Germans, the tree was always an oak. When Prince Albert, who travelled to England from Germany to marry Queen Victoria, reintroduced the idea of the Christmas tree, the oak tree had somehow turned into a fir tree. Still, it made sense. It is, after all, a darned sight easier to find a small fir tree than it is to find a small oak tree. And unless you live in a castle with massively high ceilings, it is considerably easier to fit a fir tree into your home than it would be to squeeze in an oak tree.

And so, on Christmas Eve, while Patsy finished preparing for Christmas Day, I did a final surgery before the holidays.

Unless there was a flu epidemic in the area, Christmas was usually a fairly quiet time for country doctors in the 1970s. I'm not really sure why this should have been, other than the feeling that most people were probably too busy to bother the doctor with anything trivial, or with anything which looked or felt as though it would comfortably wait until the New Year. At Christmas, no one came into the surgery wanting a medical for a job or an insurance company. Not many people turned up wanting to have repeat prescriptions for their regular medicines. Hardly anyone arrived to check on the results of an X-ray or a blood test. And, of course, there were very few holidaymakers in the area, so the population of the village was pretty well limited to the residents.

My friend William, a GP with a practice in the English Midlands, always used to say that most people were just too busy to be ill over Christmas and it wasn't as daft a thought as it might sound.

In order to minimise the number of people ringing me on Christmas Day, I always used to do one last surgery late in the afternoon on Christmas Eve, whatever day of the week it came on. Even if Christmas Eve fell on a Sunday I would do my Christmas Eve surgery. Things were sometimes so quiet that I found myself sitting in the consulting room catching up with my correspondence or sorting through other assorted paperwork. I remember I once did a Christmas Eve surgery that was attended by just three patients – and two of those only turned up to bring in bottles of home-made wine.

(Home-made wine was always a very common and popular gift in the village. Some of the wine Patsy and I were given tasted far superior to any of the expensive stuff bottled in France and sold by expensive wine merchants. Bilberry wine was always one of my favourites.)

But by no means all Christmas Eve surgeries were quiet. I remember one in particular which seemed to last for ever.

The first patient to totter in was Edward Low, a dusty and diffident old man who had celebrated his 97th birthday just three weeks earlier. There were still people in the village who referred to him as Young Mr Edward.

I always found Mr Low fascinating to talk to.

Since he was born in the 1880s, he could remember Queen Victoria's reign quite well. He was one of the few people left in England who had seen W.G.Grace play cricket. Astonishingly, Mr Low's father, also called Edward, had been born in 1802, before the battle of Trafalgar and before the battle of Waterloo. Mr Low senior had been 78-years-old when young Edward was born. His wife, young Edward's mother, had been the fifth woman to hold that obviously well-sought after position and she'd been just 29-years-old when she'd given birth. Before her marriage she had been a barmaid at the Bilbury village pub, which had been called 'The White Hart' in those days. Curiously, all of Mr Low senior's wives had been barmaids and all of them had been much younger than their husband. Three of them had died in childbirth and the fourth had died of cholera. I don't know what the fifth had died of but Mr Low was a widower when I met him.

Mr Low collected old silver and earlier in his life his enthusiasm had become an obsession, a mania which affected every aspect of his life.

He could still look at an old piece of silver, examine the hallmark and, without reference to any book of marks, tell you who had made the piece, when they had made it and where they had made it. He may have been in his 90s but he knew that for all of us it is the struggle, the competition, the hope and, perhaps the occasional success, which gives meaning and real satisfaction to our lives. He was, he once said, far too young to retire. He loved looking at old silver.

I once showed him a table spoon which Patsy and I owned and he pointed out the lion mark which proved that it was sterling silver, the initials which showed that it was made by a famous silversmith called Paul Storr, the letter 'b' which showed that it was made in the year 1817, the leopard's head which showed that it was made in London and the head of George III which showed that the duty had been paid on the spoon.

Mr Low's own impressive collection included a variety of silver items which had been discovered by a man ferreting for rabbits in a field between Bilbury and South Molton. The most prized item was a tiny bottle in a silver cage. The bottle had a small a spoon attached and was, he explained, a snuff bottle for ladies to use. They used the small spoon because it enabled them to take the snuff without getting their hands or gloves soiled or stained with the snuff powder.

I have no idea why (and nor did he) but it was apparently not at all uncommon for old silver treasures to be found in rabbit burrows. No one suspected that the rabbits had collected the items themselves and the only realistic conclusion was that thieves who were desperate to hide their 'swag' had sometimes thrust it into a rabbit hole and then been arrested or died before they could rescue it. At a place called Stoke Prior in Herefordshire a man who had been ferreting for rabbits on 16th December in 1891 found a remarkable collection of 16th and early 17th century silver. All the silver was a little dusty and tarnished but in otherwise perfect condition.

The piece de resistance in Mr Low's collection was something called a 'wager cup', a silver cup made in 1619 that was about nine inches high but which was elaborately designed and decorated. At the top of the cup there was a tiny windmill with a step ladder and upon the step ladder there was a tiny miller who was carrying a sack on his back. The cup also had working sails and a tube. The odd thing about the cup (which Mr Low told me was sold at auction as a model windmill because the auctioneer didn't recognise it for what it was) was that it could only be set down when it was empty.

'Do you know what it is?' he asked me when he showed me the item. At the time it was standing on a table and looked for all the world like a very expensive model of a windmill.

I said that I thought that it was perhaps a toy for a young aristocrat.

'It's a wager cup,' Mr Low explained. 'To fill the cup you turn it upside down and pour in your chosen beverage. You then blow down the tube. Blowing down the tube starts the sails going round. The idea is to fill the cup, blow down the tube and then empty the cup before the sails stop going round. The drinker and his companions would bet on whether or not he would succeed in doing this – and that is why it's called 'a wager cup'.'

Not surprisingly, Mr Low hadn't brought his wager cup with him when he came to my Christmas Eve surgery. I have no idea what it was worth but it wasn't the sort of thing you carted around with you for no good reason.

After sitting down and apologising for troubling me on Christmas Eve, Mr Low held out his right hand. It wasn't difficult to see what the problem was. His right thumbnail was black and there was clearly a good deal of blood gathering underneath it.

'I bet that hurts!' I said, taking a look at the thumbnail. I'd never seen anything quite so nasty looking.

'It does,' replied Mr Low, who was not a man to use 11 words when two would do just as well. (Unless he was talking about old silver.)

'How on earth did you do that?'

'Hammering.'

'What were you hammering?'

'Nail.'

'Why were you hammering a nail?'

'Put a picture up.'

'And clearly you missed.'

'I did. I intended to hit the nail.'

'When did you do it?'

'This morning.'

This was clearly not going to be one of those consultations which goes on and on. I picked a paperclip out of the little glass dish on my desk and straightened it out. I then took a lighter out of my pocket. (I always carry three things in my pockets: a penknife, a small torch and a lighter. If you light as many bonfires as I do then you always need a lighter handy.) I used the lighter to heat the end of the paperclip. This wasn't to sterilise it; I just needed the metal to be red hot.

'Give me your hand, please.'

Mr Low held out his hand.

I took hold of it, to make sure he didn't move, though I rather suspect that he wouldn't have moved whatever I did, and then I held the end of the heated paperclip against the bulging nail. The paperclip burnt quickly through the nail and the blood inside slowly trickled out, relieving the pressure inside almost instantly. I used a sterile wipe to clear away the blood and then, when the bleeding had stopped, I put a small dressing on the thumb.

'That's better,' said Mr Low with a happy smile.

'Good.'

'Merry Christmas to you and your family.'

'And a merry Christmas to you, too,' I said.

I did like Mr Low. He was very much at ease with his age; more so, I think, than any of my other patients.

'Death smiles at all of us eventually,' he once said to me. 'All we can do is smile back.'

I will always remember something else he said to me.

'It is life which so often takes away and destroys our memories,' he said. 'Death, usually considered the enemy, safeguards our memories and seals our real treasures for eternity.'

That must have been on one of his loquacious days.

He smiled, stood up and left. He was a little uncertain, and wobbled a little occasionally, but he was more alive than many people I knew who were a fraction of his age.

Amazingly, the whole consultation, including the small operation, had taken less than five minutes.

My second patient was Carlile Bentham, a man in his forties whose main problem was his weight. Well, that was his main health problem. He may well have other problems. He may have had Japanese knotweed in his garden. He may have had termites chewing up his beams.

Mr Bentham weighed as much as two ordinary men of his height and the result of effectively carrying around a spare human being was that his joints were in quite a bad way. He had terrible osteoarthritis and suffered terribly from back pain. I tried for years to help him lose weight but he was, I'm afraid, a lost cause. Whenever I tried to persuade him to follow some sort of diet, he insisted that he had abnormal glands or argued that since both his parents and both his brothers were also vastly overweight he must have been born with some genetic predisposition to obesity. He didn't seem to think it relevant that throughout their lives his parents and brothers all consumed around 6,000 calories a day a piece. Nor did he seem to be inclined to regard the knowledge that his parents both died in their 50s while his brothers didn't live to get out of their 40s as a warning.

Mr Bentham was in my surgery because he had just been discharged from hospital.

Six weeks earlier, our village postman had called in at the surgery to tell me that he'd gone to Mr Bentham's home to deliver the mail and had heard someone shouting for 'help' from an upstairs room. Not having the faintest idea what was going on I telephoned the police. Unfortunately, our resident representative of the constabulary, Police Constable Peculiar Clarke, was away on a training course in Exeter and so I had to ring 999 and ask an operator sitting in a room somewhere in Yorkshire to send someone as soon as they could.

Since I knew that it would take at least half an hour for a policeman to drive to Mr Bentham's house, I drove round there myself.

I knocked on the front door and waited. There was no response.

'Hello?' I called, rather nervously. 'Is anyone there?'

Again, there was no response.

Since the door was unlocked I took my courage in my hands and walked into the house. I called out again. Once more there was no answer.

I looked around downstairs and could find no signs of life.

So I went up the stairs, half expecting a burglar to start firing a shotgun at me as I did so.

Mr Bentham lived in one of those tiny cottages which were built in the days when people were much smaller. The staircase was one of those very steep and narrow staircases which were popular with cottage builders in the 17th century and the early parts of the 19th century. This cottage, I knew, had been built in 1834. This was not because I had any architectural expertise but because I had noticed that the date 1834 was carved into a stone block above the front door. On a long, urban road that might have been the house number. In Bilbury it was clearly the date when the cottage had been built.

There was no one in either of the bedrooms.

But I found Mr Bentham in the bathroom.

To be more precise, I found him in the bath.

He was naked, badly scalded and almost unconscious. The hot tap was still running but the plug was out and there was very little water in the bath. The only occupants were Mr Bentham and a small, yellow, rubber duck lying on its side at the tap end of the bath. I immediately turned off the tap.

This had all the makings of a real life mystery.

Why was Mr Bentham lying naked in his bath with the hot tap running but very little water around him? The water coming from the hot tap was still blisteringly hot so I assumed that instead of having a hot water storage tank, he had one of those boilers which heats up the water indefinitely.

It was the sort of puzzle that Sherlock Holmes would have welcomed on a wet, wintery afternoon.

It was clear, however, that finding the explanation would have to wait. The first thing to do was to get him out of the bath, into an ambulance and off to hospital. It was immediately clear that the scalds on his body would need professional, specialist treatment.

The only difference between a burn and a scald is that a burn is caused by dry heat (such as a fire or a hot plate) whereas a scald is caused by something wet and hot such as, well, hot water. Both burns and scalds have to be treated carefully and patiently and one of the biggest risks is the danger of infection. If I managed to get Mr Bentham out of his bath tub I feared that I would do more damage to his skin and I would dramatically increase the chance of his developing a serious infection. I did not have any of the things I would need to deal with a large scald. For a start I would really need a couple of acres of a suitable, sterile dressing. But in my bag I had a triangular bandage and a packet of sticking plasters.

But it was also clear that I would have absolutely no chance of being able to lift Mr Bentham by myself.

So that was the second problem.

I checked Mr Bentham's pulse. It seemed fine. His heart was ticking away. Apart from the scalds I could find no other signs of problems. However, he felt cold. I plucked a large towel from a rack and lay it over his body. It didn't come anywhere to covering him. I fetched an eiderdown from a bedroom and put that over him. I then telephoned for an ambulance.

'You don't need to send the police car now,' I told the operator, when I'd asked for an ambulance to be sent.

'They're already on their way,' she said. 'Someone called them a short while ago.'

'That was me,' I said. 'But I don't need them now.'

'But they have to come out if they've been called,' insisted the operator.

It occurred to me that we would probably be able to use their muscle in helping to move Mr Bentham from his bathroom to the ambulance so I just thanked her very much and replaced the telephone receiver.

Now that I knew what the problem was, I was beginning to worry a good deal about the logistics of how we were going to move a badly scalded 25 stone man out of his bathroom and down his very narrow, very steep stairs. Those cottage stairs used to cause me a lot of problems. Mr Bentham's stairs were, if anything, narrower and steeper than the stairs in the cottages belonging to any of my other patients.

I hoped that the police might send a car with two occupants. Maybe the two police officers and the two ambulance paramedics might manage to lift him.

'Mr Bentham?' I said, for the umpteenth time. 'Can you hear me?'

It had occurred to me that he might have got into the bath, slipped and banged his head. Or that he might have suffered a stroke.

Suddenly, Mr Bentham opened his eyes. He looked at me and frowned.

'Is that you, doctor?'

I asked him what had happened and he slowly explained that he'd prepared his bath, half filling it with water, and then climbed in. Deciding that the water wasn't hot enough he had reached forward and turned off the cold tap and, at more or less the same time, turned the hot tap on full.

It was while doing this that his back had gone into spasm. Unable to move he had lain there in the bath, immersed in water that was getting hotter and hotter by the minute. When the bath was full, the excess water flowed out through the overflow but since the hot water was still coming in, the result was that the temperature of the water just increased until it was unbearable.

156

Unable to lean forwards to reach the taps, he had had the presence of mind to use one of his feet to pull at the chain holding the bath plug in place. And he had succeeded in removing the plug.

Unfortunately, by this time he was badly scalded.

And since his back was in spasm he couldn't get out of the bath to walk into his bedroom to telephone for help. In fact, he hadn't been able to get out of the bath at all.

'Can you stand up?' I asked him.

He made a feeble attempt to stand. It was a failure. Moreover, when he tried to move, it was clear that the badly scalded parts of his skin were stuck to the bath. When he moved he was pulling skin away from the enamel.

'I'm in far too much pain, doctor,' he said. He had tears in his eyes and I don't blame him. If I'd been in his skin I'd have had tears in my eyes too. The scalds I could see looked incredibly painful. His feet, legs, and bottom were the worst.

I stayed with him while I waited for the police and the ambulance crew to arrive and while I waited I telephoned Bilbury Grange to explain where I was and that I was likely to be there for some time. I also asked Patsy to ring her father for me. It seemed to me that we were likely to need his help too.

It took the emergency services just under an hour to get to Bilbury and those sixty minutes seemed interminable. Mr Bentham was clearly in a good deal of pain, both with the original back trouble and with the scalds from the hot water and so I gave him an injection of morphine. He relaxed then and drifted off to sleep. While he slept I used an indelible felt tip pen to write a big M on his forehead. I wrote beside it the dosage I'd given him. I needed to be sure that the doctors at the hospital knew that Mr Bentham had been given morphine. I could have written the details on a note, or simply told the ambulance crew. But this way there was no bit of paper to lose and no need for me to worry about someone forgetting to pass on the message.

The ambulance arrived first (in my experience if you ring for the police and for an ambulance at the same time it is nearly always the ambulance which arrives first) and the police arrived about two minutes later. There were two men in the ambulance crew and two men in the police car. All looked to be fairly strong, meaty looking fellows. I went down, met them, explained what the problem was and then led them upstairs.

'So, how do we get him downstairs?' asked the older of the two ambulance men. 'Is there a coffin window anywhere?'

The younger ambulance man looked at him as if he were stark raving mad. 'What the devil is a coffin window?'

'In those old cottages with steep, narrow staircases they used to have one window that was big enough to get a coffin through,' explained the older ambulance man. He wandered into the two tiny bedrooms and came back a moment later looking very glum.

'There isn't one,' he announced.

I already knew this because I had looked, but in my experience it is, in such circumstances, always better to let the professionals find such things out for themselves. I had also had time to work out that if we were going to take Mr Bentham out through a window then we were probably going to have to remove the window frame and, quite possibly, a row or two of bricks.

The younger ambulance man lifted the eiderdown which was covering Mr Bentham and shook his shoulder. 'Can you stand up?'

Mr Bentham didn't wake up and didn't respond.

'I gave him some morphine,' I explained. 'He's badly scalded.'

'How the devil did it happen?' asked the older ambulance man.

I explained.

'Is there any question of foul play?' asked one of the policemen. It was the first time either of them had spoken. If they were wondering why they'd been called neither of them said so. The two policemen looked to be approximately the same age but one of them had long, bushy sideburns and a moustache and the other didn't. The one who spoke was the one without a moustache.

'No, I don't think so,' I said.

'But you don't know so?'

'I'm pretty sure there is no question of foul play.'

'Nevertheless, with respect doctor, maybe we should treat this as a crime scene,' said the policeman without a moustache.

'I think we ought to get my patient to hospital before we worry about anything else,' I pointed out.

The policeman, who looked unconvinced and a trifle unhappy, eventually agreed that moving Mr Bentham out of his bathroom should take precedence over everything else.

'So how are we going to move him?' asked the policeman who did have a moustache.

'Can we lift him?' asked one of the ambulance men. He bent down and tried pulling Mr Bentham up out of the bath. Mr Bentham groaned but didn't wake. 'Strewth,' he said. 'He's stuck to the bath!'

'How much does he weigh?' asked the other ambulance man.

'Around 25 stone,' I replied.

The two ambulance men then tried to lift Mr Bentham up so that they could put him onto a stretcher. One side of the bath was up against the wall and so the two men had to stand on the same side of the bath to do their lifting. I squeezed in alongside them and we all tried to lift together. We couldn't budge him. And it was clear that because his skin was stuck to the bath we were pulling off skin every time we tried to move him.

There was much tutting and shaking of heads. The policeman with the moustache mentioned that he had a bad back and had been told by his doctor not to do any heavy lifting.

'Maybe it would be easier to move him and the bath together,' I suggested.

The four men looked at me as if I were mad.

'Well, I don't think we are going to be able to lift him out of the bath without some sort of hoist',' I pointed out. 'And we don't have a hoist. Do we?'

They all shook their heads.

'If we could drag the bath to the top of the stairs we could perhaps sort of slide him and the bath down the stairs,' suggested the policeman with the moustache and the bad back.

We all contemplated this suggestion.

'He'd be travelling at a fair old lick by the time he reached the bottom of the stairs,' said the policeman without a moustache.

'Probably go straight through the floorboards,' said the younger ambulance man. 'Straight down into the cellar. Then we'd have to get him out of the cellar.'

'These cottages don't have cellars,' pointed out to his colleague. 'Solid floors.'

'It'll have to be the window,' I said, indicating the small bathroom window. The window was about two feet square.

'Nowhere near big enough,' said the policeman with the moustache.

159

'We'll have to take the frame out and remove some bricks,' said the older ambulance man. 'I remember we did something similar with a chap in Barnstaple a few years back. He weighed 30 stone and needed to go into hospital. He was sleeping in a big chair downstairs but we couldn't lift him so we took out some bricks and drove a fork lift truck into the room to lift him up and carry him out. We lifted him and the chair together.'

'We're on the first floor here,' the younger ambulance man reminded his colleague.

The four of them were still considering the situation when I heard what sounded like a tractor approaching. I had never before been so pleased to hear the sound of a tractor. I went to the little window and looked out. Down below, parked behind the ambulance and the police car which were blocking the lane, was Mr Kennet, my father-in-law. He was driving a huge, red tractor which was equipped with two large forks or prongs at the front. Normally used for moving hay bales these prongs would, I thought, be perfectly capable of moving a bath containing a large man.

And that is exactly how we moved Mr Bentham out of his bathroom.

The two policemen found a sledge hammer and an axe in Mr Bentham's shed (I idly wondered how long it had been since Mr Bentham himself had been able to use either of those) and the policeman who didn't have the bad back and the younger ambulance man used them to remove the window, the window frame and several rows of bricks. Eventually, they created a hole big enough to allow the bath and Mr Bentham to pass through. While they did this, the policeman with the bad back and the moustache managed to find a wrench. He turned off the water and then disconnected the two taps and the pipe which took dirty water from the bath to the cottage drains.

It took nearly three hours to extricate Mr Bentham and his bath from the bathroom and before then I had to give him another morphine injection to keep him comfortable.

'We're going to take you to hospital in Barnstaple,' I told him, when he had woken up, jolted by the ambulance men and the policemen pushing and dragging the bath and its human contents a little closer to the window.

'Is it all right if we make some necessary structural amendments to your bathroom wall?' shouted one of the policemen who was clearly one of those people who assumes that all people who are elderly, ill or in some way incapacitated are also deaf. I did wonder why he had bothered to ask this since the amendments had already been made.

Mr Bentham, who was in a considerable amount of pain and heavily drugged, didn't know where he was or even who he was and probably couldn't have given a sensible response to any question he was asked. He stared at the policeman, mumbled something incomprehensible and closed his eyes again.

Eventually, Mr Kennet managed to get the forks at the front of his tractor safely underneath the bath. We then watched, with some apprehension, as he backed the tractor away from the hole in the bathroom wall, over the flower bed and rhododendron bush (which the tractor had already flattened on its way in) and back towards the lane. We continued to watch nervously as the tractor wobbled over the now rutted garden, and for a moment I thought the weight of the bath and Mr Bentham was going to prove too much for it. But tractors are sturdy vehicles and we breathed a little easier as Mr Kennet slowly managed to wobble and sway through the remains of the small wall and the wooden gate (which he had pretty well destroyed on his way in towards the cottage) and out into the lane.

It proved impossible to manipulate the bath into the back of the ambulance without first lowering it onto the ground and then lifting it so that it lay across the prongs in a north and south direction, rather than an east and west direction. And despite his skills Mr Kennet wasn't able to put the bath into the back of the ambulance without accidentally removing one of the vehicle's doors and damaging the other one beyond repair. Tractors aren't built for fine work – particularly when they are operating on uneven ground.

Four and a half hours after the postman had called in at Bilbury Grange, we finally managed to send Mr Bentham on his way to hospital in Barnstaple. The two policemen, the two ambulance men, Mr Kennet and I were all absolutely exhausted.

And when the ambulance arrived at the hospital it apparently took the staff there another two and a half hours to extricate the bath from the back of the ambulance and Mr Bentham from the bath.

The ambulance was too badly damaged to be repaired, the bath was destroyed and the police sent a firm of builders from Barnstaple to fix a tarpaulin over the hole in the wall of Mr Bentham's cottage. The damaged wall and the broken gate they left for another day. The poor rhododendron bush, which had fallen in the battle of Mr Bentham's Bath, was a permanent casualty and beyond hope.

But Mr Bentham, I'm pleased to say, made a complete recovery. His scalds were treated and when he left hospital six weeks or so later he was able to walk with the aid of nothing more than a walking stick. To everyone's surprise he managed to put on half a stone during his stay in hospital and he was said to be the only patient in history to have gained weight while eating hospital food.

And now he was back sitting in my surgery.

His scalds were more or less mended and he told me that the police and the ambulance service had agreed to pay for the repairs to his cottage and garden and that his lawyer had advised him against taking additional legal action for damages. He said that his lawyer had persuaded the NHS to install a stairlift into his cottage and had provided him with a specially adapted electrically powered invalid chair so that he could get about the village. He wasn't disabled but his immense bulk meant that he found it difficult to walk more than a few yards.

'And I decided not to sue you,' he told me, as though this were an immense favour.

'Thank you,' I said. 'That's very kind of you.' I tried not to sound sarcastic though it wasn't easy.

'My lawyer said you probably acted as you thought best.'

I nodded.

'And my solicitor says that it probably isn't worth suing a country doctor anyway.'

'That's good of him.'

'He says country doctors like you don't have much money.'

'Well, he's right about that.'

'So you might not even be able to pay his costs and I could end up out of pocket.'

I was surprised that the solicitor didn't know that all doctors have insurance to protect them against patients who turned into litigants. Still, I was glad I didn't have to deal with a lawsuit.

I idly wondered if Mr Bentham might get around to thanking me for getting him to the hospital.

'I'm having a shower put into the bathroom; instead of the bath.'

'That sounds like a good idea.'

'The NHS and the police are paying so I'm having the very best. And I'm having the bathroom retiled.'

I realised that the moment had long past. He wasn't going to say thank you because he didn't think he had anything to thank me for.

'I thought I might consider losing a little weight in the New Year,' he then added, as though he felt he were doing me a favour.

'That might be wise,' I said. I didn't have much hope that this would turn out to be anything other than yet another empty hope.

The Daily Express newspaper wants to run a series of articles about my weight loss. They've hired a famous dietician to be my personal adviser.'

'Splendid!'

'So can you weigh me, please? They need to know how much I weigh now.'

'I'm afraid I can't.'

He frowned. 'Why not?'

'Because my scales only go up to 20 stone and according to the letter I had about you from the hospital you now weigh nearly 26 stone.'

'Then how do I get weighed?'

I suggested that he might contact the hospital to see if he could get weighed on their scales. 'Otherwise,' I said, 'you could just lose some weight and then when you're a bit thinner we could start weighing you here.'

He didn't look very happy about this.

'I'm sorry,' I said, though I wasn't quite sure why I was apologising.

'And I need a sick note,' he said. 'The doctor at the hospital gave me one but it expires tomorrow.'

Mr Bentham had not been to work for as long as I'd been in Bilbury. As far as I knew he had never worked. Since it was clear that he was never likely to look for a job, let alone find one, I usually gave him a sick note for six months.

'And tomorrow is Christmas Day, so you need the note today?'

'Yes.'

I wrote out a sick note for six months and handed it to him.

He stood up, and waddled towards the door.

'Happy Christmas!' I said.

He turned, looked at me and nodded his thanks. He didn't say Happy Christmas or anything else seasonal. 'I could have demanded that you visit me at home to give me a sick note,' he said. 'But since it's Christmas I thought I'd come to the surgery. I drove here in my invalid chair.'

I found myself thanking him again.

'And anyway I needed to go to Peter Marshall's shop to buy some supplies,' he added. 'I've ordered a couple of his Christmas hampers.'

And then, without another word, he left.

I hoped he enjoyed making his Christmas pudding and playing with the little budgie bells I knew he'd find in his Peter Marshall hampers.

I confess I felt relieved that I didn't have any other patients like Mr Bentham.

My next patient was Miss Brunehilda Tyneham; a woman who was in her late 60s and something of a celebrity in the village.

Miss Tyneham was renowned for the column she wrote for a local paper called the *Barnstaple, Bideford and Bilbury Herald*. When the editor had originally commissioned the column he had, I suspect, asked Miss Tyneham to send in reports of events in the village which might otherwise have been missed by the paper's reporting staff. Local newspapers often fill their columns with reports of this type – usually detailing meetings of the Women's Institute, flower and vegetable show results and the successes or failures of the local sports teams.

However, Miss Tyneham's column had slowly changed and now, two decades after its inception, it had become a very personal account of her life in the village. Miss Tyneham described her garden, her experiences with local builders, her dissatisfactions with the council and so on. There was very little space left for details of jam making competitions or other local events. Miss Tyneham was famous for her strange use of words, for her mistakes and for her misprints. Once, in an obituary she published about an elderly villager, she had included the line: 'She pissed away peacefully in her sleep'. Miss Tyneham, mortally embarrassed, blamed the printers. They claimed the error was hers. The misprint became a classic and was widely quoted in books about journalism.

Although still relatively young in Bilbury terms (I had a number of patients who were well over 80, quite a few who were in their 90s and one or two who had already celebrated their 100th birthdays and had received their congratulatory telegrams from Her Majesty the Queen constantly on display on their mantelpiece) Miss Tyneham had not allowed her relative youth to delay her acquiring the occasionally impatient and acerbic manner sometimes observed among those who have reached an age where they, quite rightly, feel that they have earned the right to speak their mind.

'The old are different to other people,' Miss Tyneham once said to me. 'They have mostly experienced stresses, frustrations, failures and disappointments for many years. Some have begun to expect disappointment and most realise that each day will invariably bring another round of unexpected hazards into their lives. Moreover, they see the next generation, and the generation after that, making the same silly mistakes that they made and that can be damnably infuriating. At a certain age most people realise that no one ever learns from the past and that can be quite exhausting.'

Having marched into the surgery as if she were going to war, Miss Tyneham pointed her black, silk umbrella at me. 'I require to have full and discursive intercourse with you, doctor,' she said. For a moment I thought she was about to poke me in the chest with the umbrella. 'And I shall require your full attention throughout.' I noticed that although she had marched into the room she had limped slightly. And I could see that there was a bandage around her left ankle.

'I am at your service, Miss Tyneham,' I replied.

Whenever I spoke to her I always felt as if I had been dragged back into Victorian times. I knew that whatever it was which had brought her to the surgery would have to wait until she had had a little rant about something which had annoyed her. I didn't mind. To be honest, I always found her rants quite entertaining.

'I had a social worker come to see me this past week,' said Miss Tyneham, and it was immediately clear that this was not the prelude to a complimentary remark but the beginning of a complaint.

'Ah!' I said. I knew better than to commit myself to an opinion on the event at this early stage in the conversation.

'She wanted to help me!'

I knew immediately that this was going to be a complaint.

'She told me that loneliness is bad for one. She said that being lonely is as harmful as smoking a pack of cigarettes a day. Do you agree with that?'

'I'm not sure,' I replied, rather taken aback.

'She wanted to send people in to talk to me occasionally! Me!'

'Ah.'

'She wanted to send round volunteer visitors. Strangers to talk to me, drink my tea, eat my biscuits and meddle. Can you imagine?' She leant forwards and glowered. 'Did you send her?'

'No, certainly not. I didn't send her.'

'I told her that I don't smoke so I'll take my chances with the loneliness,' said Miss Tyneham. 'I like being alone.'

'I understand,' I said. 'I didn't ask anyone to call.'

'Why do people under 40 always assume that anyone over 60 must be senile, and then act surprised and delighted when they turn out not to be?'

'I don't know.'

'And why am I invisible in shops?' she demanded.

Miss Tyneham was now in full flow.

'I stood at the counter in the Post Office the other day,' she said, 'and a girl of about 18 came up, completely ignored me, and asked for a book of stamps. She and the fellow behind the counter behaved as though I were completely invisible. They just chatted away as if I weren't there at all. When the girl had finished and had tottered off, I asked the man behind the glass if I could have my turn. I said 'I'm sorry I'm not 18 and wearing a tight top but am I still allowed to buy stamps?' He looked at me as if I were barking mad, closed his partition and disappeared so I obviously really was invisible.' She leant forwards and raised her voice. 'Can you see me sitting here?'

'I certainly can.'

'Good. That's good.'

I waited. I knew that she would tell me why she had come when she was ready.

'I knocked my ankle,' she announced.

'Let me see.'

'You want to see it?'

'Yes, please.'

'To look at my leg?'

'Yes.'

'Here it is.' She moved her leg to show me the bandaged ankle.

'I'll need to see it without the bandage.'

'I would have to remove my stocking.'

'Yes, you would.'

'Look away.'

'You can go behind the examination screen.'

'There's no need for that if you look away.'

I turned my head and looked out of the French windows. Two squirrels were chasing each other round and round on the lawn. I watched them for a while.

'Well, are you going to look at my leg or not?'

I turned back.

Miss Tyneham had rolled her stocking down and had removed the bandage from her ankle.

'What happened?'

'I knocked myself on a table leg.'

She had clearly been bitten by a dog. There were distinct signs of two teeth marks in her skin. The wound was infected.

I looked at her and raised an eyebrow. She went red. And then a tear slowly formed in her left eye and started to roll down her cheek.

'Did Fluffy do that?' I asked.

I knew that she had a small Dandie Dinmont terrier called Fluffy. She and the dog were inseparable and had been partners in life for years.

'Was it Fluffy who bit you?' I wanted to ask why she hadn't come to see me before. But I knew the answer to that. She was worried that Fluffy might get into trouble.

'Will they destroy her?'

'Will who destroy her?'

'The authorities. The police.'

'Why should anyone destroy her?'

'She bit me. I trod on her paw by accident. She didn't mean to bite me. I know she didn't mean to bite me.' She paused and cleared her throat. 'They put dogs down if they bite people, don't they?' The last bit came out as a whisper.

'Are you going to tell the police that Fluffy bit you?'

'Of course not!'

'Is Fluffy going to confess? Get tiddly in the pub and tell his mates about it?'

'No, of course he isn't. He's not that sort of dog.' Another tear joined the first one.

'Does anyone else know she bit you?' I handed Miss Tyneham a paper handkerchief. She dabbed at her cheeks.

'No!'

'Well, I'm certainly not going to tell them,' I assured her. 'So it seems as though Fluffy's secret is safe with us.'

I gave a suitable injection, cleaned up the wound, dealt with the damage and put in a couple of stitches. I told Miss Tyneham to come back to see me in five days so that I could take a look at how the wound was healing. Finally, I handed her a packet of antibiotics and gave her instructions on how to take them.

'Bless you, doctor,' she said. She wiped away more tears. 'Thank you.'

She rolled up her stocking and fastened it while I scribbled a note in her records. When we had both finished I showed her what I'd written.

'I haven't mentioned Fluffy in my records,' I said. 'It just says 'bitten by unknown dog'.'

She didn't say anything for a moment. She put the antibiotics and the tissue into her handbag and then, when she had composed herself she stood up and headed for the door. 'Happy Christmas, doctor!'

'Happy Christmas, Miss Tyneham.'

'Thank you,' she whispered.

And then she left.

My next three patients weren't ill at all. They had all brought small gifts. And all the gifts were home-made.

Iolanthe Fielding had brought Patsy and me a Christmas gift of home-made mince pies. She stressed that although she had made the pies, the gift came from both her and her husband.

Mrs Westingham, who was waiting patiently for an operation on her bilateral cataracts, had brought a card which she had embroidered herself. The words on the card seemed to be 'Merry Cristmos and a Hoppy New Year' but although there might have been some question about the spelling the sentiment was beyond dispute.

We were lucky enough to receive an enormous quantity of cards from patients (including one from Mrs Peters with a photo of herself half way up her cherry tree on the front) but there could be no doubt that Mrs Westingham's contribution would have pride of place in the middle of the dining room mantelpiece. She must have spent hours working on the embroidered message.

And Mr and Mrs Fothergill had brought a bottle of their home-made elderberry and carrot wine. I once made the mistake of drinking two glasses of their elderberry and carrot creation when Mr Fothergill was at home in bed recovering from a haemorrhoid operation. I was woozy for several hours afterwards. It is a potent but palatable brew.

And so the Christmas Eve surgery finished in fine style.

But Christmas had one more surprise for me.

Sitting in the kitchen, with Patsy and a good part of our menagerie were Harry Stottle and Mildred Snodgrass (aka 'Melina Melons').

'We have received gifts,' I said, when I'd greeted everyone. I put the box of mince pies, the bottle of wine and the hand embroidered card down on the table. 'The pies are from Mr and Mrs Fielding, the wine is from Mr and Mrs Fothergill and the card was handmade by Mrs Westingham whose cataracts are clearly just about ready for removal.'

Patsy told me that the children were already safely tucked up in bed and so after saying a quick 'hello' I hurried upstairs to say goodnight and to suggest, quite pointlessly, that they didn't burst into our bedroom before 6.00 am if at all possible.

And then I head back downstairs.

Patsy and our visitors looked as if they had eaten all the cream – including the cat's share. Harry, normally a fairly phlegmatic character, too cool for the icebox, looked as if he were about to burst with excitement. Mildred, who was, as one might expect from her choice of profession, a well-built and shapely woman with an ebullient personality, was holding his arm as though frightened that he might otherwise blow away. She was wearing a tight, red dress which was trimmed with faux, white fur and, just in case the seasonal references were to be missed, she had a sprig of mistletoe in

169

her hair. The gods had definitely not skimped when they had glued her together. Patsy was smiling and clearly had a secret to share.

'We have news,' said Harry.

'The good variety, I hope,' I said.

'Absolutely!' said Mildred. She let out a little yelp of excitement, as though someone had just pinched her bottom. But they hadn't. I knew this because I could see both of Harry's hands.

'Mildred and Harry have an announcement to make,' said Patsy. She and Mildred went to school together and had remained chums.

'Mildred has consented to be my wife,' said Harry with a huge grin. 'We're planning a big wedding with the reception at the Duck and Puddle.'

'And afterwards I expect I shall have to just lie back and think of England!' said Mildred, with a giggle. She rolled her eyes in mock horror.

'In that case, I shall address you as 'Your Ladyship',' said Harry.

Puzzled, Mildred looked at him.

'Lady Hillingdon was the woman who first mentioned lying back and thinking of England in the bedroom,' explained Harry.

Mildred looked delighted. 'My Harry knows all sorts of stuff!' she said proudly. She looked at me. 'Isn't it amazing that my Harry is a doctor too, like you! You could have knocked me down with a feather when he told me that! I thought he was a barman but he's a psychiatrist as well. He can probably look right into my mind and know exactly what I'm thinking.' She giggled and stuck an elbow into his ribs. 'You keep out of my mind you dirty old devil!'

'We're going to see the vicar of St Dympnas after Christmas,' said Harry, who was, to my astonishment, now looking slightly embarrassed. I'd never seen him look nonplussed let alone embarrassed. Mind you, I'd never heard him described as 'a dirty old devil' before. And it probably wasn't a phrase commonly used about him either by his celebrity patients or the medical students he taught.

'Patsy is going to be my maid of honour,' announced Mildred. 'And I'm going to ask Adrienne, Gilly, Anne and Carole to be my bridesmaids.'

Adrienne was Patsy's sister and Patchy Fogg's wife. Gilly Parsons was married to Frank and they ran the Duck and Puddle together. Anne, the former Anne Thwaites, was married to Thumper

Robinson. And Carole was Carole Singer – and, as far as I knew, Bilbury's only other professional ecdysiast.

This was clearly going to be a wedding and a half.

'It's time I gave up work so I'll be hanging up my nipple tassles,' said Mildred. 'I can't be 19 much longer. When I got to 35 I said I'd push my age up to 25 but there's a limited market for 25-year-olds so I slipped down a rainbow and went back to 19.' She giggled.

'And I'd like you to be my best man,' Harry said to me.

'Oh, please say 'yes'!' said Mildred. 'You have to say 'yes'!'

'Would you like the mince pies cold?' I asked. 'Or shall I pop them in the oven?'

'Oh, let's put them in the oven,' said Patsy. She put the mince pies onto a suitable plate and popped them into the ever warm AGA.

'Say 'yes'!' said Mildred. 'Please, please, please! I can't tell you how excited I am. I'm going to wear a big, puffy, white dress and a veil and I'll be able to have photographs taken with my clothes on! It's positively ages since anyone took my picture with me wearing undies and clothes and everything.'

In addition to taking off her clothes in public houses, Mildred was also a popular photographic model, regularly starring in the type of men's magazines which tend to carry more photographs than text and wherein she was, of course, known by her stage name of 'Melina Melons'.

I looked at Mildred, then at Harry and then at Patsy. They were all looking at me, waiting for a response to Harry's question. I couldn't help wondering what excitements awaited us. Weddings in Bilbury always seemed to be rather more eventful than any I'd ever attended elsewhere. I suspected that the wedding of Mildred Snodgrass and Ronald Eckersley (or was it Melina Melons and Harry Stottle?) was going to be quite an event.

'You get some plates and I'll get the glasses,' I said, taking out my penknife. I opened the corkscrew blade and started to remove the cork from the bottle of elderberry and carrot wine which Mr and Mrs Fothergill had brought. As I did this I looked around. Everyone still seemed to be waiting for me to say something else.

I slowly screwed the corkscrew into the cork and gently pulled. The cork slid smoothly from the bottle. 'This seems as good a way as any to celebrate my new position,' I said, with a grin, holding up the bottle and then putting it down in the middle of the table. I wandered to the cupboard where we keep our drinking glasses, found four that were almost matching, and put them down. I paused and smiled as I poured out the wine and handed round the glasses. 'I will be honoured to accept your invitation,' I said to Harry. 'I'll be thrilled to be your best man.'

And I absolutely was.

Much hugging was then done and congratulations were again offered and accepted and then we drank to Mildred and Harry and we munched mince pies and we talked of things past, present and future.

It wasn't a bad way to start our Christmas celebrations.

Author's Note

Thank you for your company. I hope you have enjoyed reading about our life in Bilbury as much as I've enjoyed recalling these memories. If you did enjoy *Bilbury Memories* I would be very grateful if you would spare a moment to write a short review. It really does help enormously.

Thank you

Vernon Coleman

P.S. Five appendices follow. I very much hope you enjoy these too.

Appendix 1: "Wolverhampton'! Stop doing that to 'Knights in the Bottom'!'

A number of media couples have named their child (or children) after the place (or places) where the conception (or conceptions) took place. In the memory entitled 'The Bucket Lists' I explained how this phenomenon had arrived in Bilbury.

This curious habit is undoubtedly now spreading and it is now increasingly common for parents to eschew traditional names and, instead, to name their offspring after the place where the child was conceived.

I don't suppose many individuals will complain overly much if they grow up being called 'Paris', 'London', 'Washington' or 'Dallas'.

But parents need to take care if they are to avoid giving their child a name which produces a lifetime of funny looks and giggles, and turns form filling into a never-ending nightmare. Here is a list of 24 places (12 in Britain and 12 in the United States) which couples intent on procreation might like to consider avoiding if they are planning to name their child in this way:

Wolverhampton, West Midlands
Stoke Mandeville, Buckinghamshire
Llandrindod Wells, Powys
Brown Willy, Cornwall
Cockup, Cumbria,
Nether Wallop, Hampshire
Pratt's Bottom, Kent
Nob End, Lancashire
Scratchy Bottom, Dorset
Bullyhole Bottom, Monmouthshire
Bishops Itchington, Staffordshire
Boggy Bottom, Hertfordshire

Knights in the Bottom, Dorset

And here are a few places that American couples contemplating parenthood might like to avoid:

Toad suck, Arizona
Oral, South Dakota
Paint lick, Kentucky
Two egg, Florida
Suckerville, Maine
Gas, Kansas
Climax, Michigan
Embarrass, Minnesota
Concrete, Washington
Whynot, North Carolina
Uncertain, Texas
Colon, Michigan,
Pink, Oklahoma
Hooker, Oklahoma

Finally, romantic couples wanting to start a family in Wales would be wise to avoid the village of Llanfairpwllgwyngyllgogerychwyndrobwillantysiliogogogoch.

Appendix 2: Loving Animals

Animal abusers argue that animals which seem to show love are merely acting according to their instincts. However, the evidence proves that animals are perfectly capable of feeling complex emotions. Animals are certainly capable of loving. Many animals are so loyal to one another that if one half of a couple dies, the other may die shortly afterwards – consumed by grief. This has been reported to happen with swans, wolves and oxen.

Here are some examples of loving animals:

1) A statue of a small Akita dog named Hachiko stands prominently in the forecourt of Japan's busiest railway station. Every morning, Hachiko would accompany his master to his train to work and arrive again at the end of the day to greet his master from his return journey. Sadly, Hachiko's master did not make the return journey one evening because he had suffered a fatal heart attack while at work. But Hachiko still waited patiently for his master to return. Hachiko returned at the same time the following day in the hope that his master would step off the train to greet him. Hachiko soon became well-known to local commuters who would often stop to lavish affection on the dog and give him treats. For an incredible nine years, Hachiko waited every evening in the hope that his master would return. When Hachiko died, the Japanese erected a statue of him in his honour to commemorate his love and devotion.

2) A Friesian cow called Daisy was sold for auction in Okehampton in Devon, England. Daisy was so upset about being parted from her new calf that she jumped over her enclosure and ran the six miles back home to be with her calf.

3) A cow called Emma was so distraught that her calf had been taken away from her that she made it her mission to find her baby. Just before milking time, Emma escaped from the field where she was kept and ran the four miles to the abattoir where her calf was about to be slaughtered. She made such a fuss when she got there

that staff admitted to being afraid. Suddenly, one of the calves in line to be slaughtered recognised its mother's cries and ran frantically towards her. Emma was so happy to be reunited with her calf that she couldn't stop licking and nuzzling her baby. Touched by what had happened, the abattoir workers contacted Emma's owner who took pity on the mother and calf and decided to keep them both.

4) In 1988, Molly Parfett's husband died in hospital after suffering from a massive stroke. Shortly after the funeral, Molly noticed that their dog, Joe, would disappear for hours at a time. She discovered that Joe was to be found sitting by his master's grave. Molly had no idea how Joe knew where her husband was buried.

5) There is a monument near Derwent Dam in Derbyshire, England, with the following inscription: 'In Commemoration of the devotion of Tip the sheepdog who stayed by the body of her dead master, Mr Joseph Tagg, on the Howden Moor for fifteen weeks from 12th December 1953 to 27th March 1954.'

6) Farmer Alfred Gruenemeyer, who lived near Coburg in central Germany, treated his animals more like pets than livestock. And so when Gruenemeyer died, his animals were devastated. A young bull called Barnaby was so distressed that he left his field, walked for a mile, leapt the cemetery wall, found the farmer's grave and started a vigil which lasted for several days. Attempts to chase the young bull away failed when locals discovered just how unnerving an angry bull can be. It wasn't until several days later that the bull calmed down and could be led back to his pasture. Mr Gruenemeyer was said by neighbours to have allowed his animals to roam in and out of his house. 'He talked to them like Dr Dolittle,' said one neighbour. 'Mind you, his house smelled a bit.'

Taken from *The Wisdom of Animals* by Vernon Coleman and Donna Antoinette Coleman (which is available as an ebook on Amazon.)

Appendix 3: Patents

In the memory about Diggory Cholmondelay, I described how Diggory's eccentric father had enthusiastically tried to promote an eating machine. The history books are surprisingly full of unusual inventions – for all of which the inventors doubtless had great hopes (especially if they dreamt them up in the middle of the night when critical faculties tend to be at their weakest).

Here are a dozen more inventions which, when looked at in the cold light of day, don't perhaps quite have the hope of the paperclip or the commercial possibilities of a pencil with an eraser fixed onto the end:

In 1915, Frank Marcovsky obtained a US Patent for a suit of protective armour designed to be worn by cyclists. The armour, which was inflated with an ordinary bicycle pump, consisted of a suit which would ensure that if the cyclist fell off his machine he would bounce to safety without any harm having been done.

In 1927, a Frenchman called Pierre Leon Martin Victor Calmels obtained a US patent for an apparatus designed to make it easier for a moustache owner to trim his pride and joy and to produce a perfectly balanced moustache.

In 1903, Joseph Karwowski obtained a US Patent for his method of preserving the dead. The idea was to encase the 'recently deceased' within a block of molten glass so that the body could be preserved indefinitely without decaying. Poorer folk, or those with less display space available, could have just the head preserved.

In 1995, Nicole M Dubus and Susan Springfield obtained a US Patent for a fork with a built in timer which would tell the eater when to take their next mouthful of food. The fork had a small light and a beeper in the handle. Diners ate only when the light in their fork changed from red to green. (It occurred to me that a drinking glass similarly equipped with red and green lights might prove useful to those struggling to moderate their drinking.)

In 1896, J.C.Boyle obtained a US Patent for a 'polite hat lifting device' which would enable men to raise their hats to ladies even if they were carrying bags or parcels. If the hat wearer bowed forwards slightly, a spring-driven mechanism would gently raise the hat, rotate it once and then replace it.

In 1879, Benjamin B Oppenheimer obtained a US Patent for a device designed to enable men and women to jump to safety from tall buildings which were on fire. A parachute built into a helmet was designed to slow down the unfortunate individual's descent to the ground. The helmet and its parachute were attached to the body by a chin strap.

In 1923, C.G.Purdy obtained a US Patent for a tooth and gum exercising device which consisted of a strong spring with small plates at each end. To use the device two people sat or stood facing each other. Each placed one of the plates in their mouth. And then both pulled – as in a tug of war.

In 1895, A.Eustis obtained a US Patent for a device designed to help servants push infirm individuals up stairs. The device consisted of a large pad, which was placed against the back of the infirm person, and two rods, attached to the pad. A healthy, young servant would then take hold of the two rods and push. The device enabled the servant to help the infirm individual up the stairs without having to touch them in which might be considered indelicate.

In 1896, Martin Goetze obtained a US Patent for a device designed to produce dimples. The device consisted of a small massage knob, which was placed in the position where the dimple was required, and a massage cylinder which had to be manually turned around the place to be dimpled.

In 1915, Lili Aline McGrath obtained a US Patent for a pair of slippers to be used as a floor polisher. The soles of the slippers were suitable for polishing and the slippers themselves were connected by a cord which was long enough to enable the wearer to take a full stride, but not long enough to allow the legs to spread wide. The inventor asserted that her device would enable the user to polish the floor while 'dancing' without any risk of falling.

In 1913, Alfred Clark obtained a US Patent for a rocking chair fitted with an attachment which enabled the user to churn butter while idly rocking away the day.

In 1866, Julian A Fogg obtained a US Patent for an improved coffin. Mr Fogg's coffin was designed to enable mourners, and curious sight seers, to view the deceased through a window in the lid.

There are more details of these inventions in a book entitled *Patently Absurd* by Christopher Cooper.

Appendix 4: The Twelve Oddest English Eccentrics

Eccentricity is an essentially English phenomenon. It is something the English always seemed to do particularly well.

But true eccentricity is something innate, rather than manufactured.

Exhibitionists, and those hoping to break into some branch of show-business, will frequently adopt some carefully thought-out form of dress or behaviour in order to draw attention to themselves. That is not eccentricity and they are not eccentrics.

Nor are the individuals who dream up stunts to get themselves into the *Guinness Book of Records* 'eccentric'.

Simply being frugal, living way beneath or beyond your means or choosing to live the life of a hermit may be odd but it isn't truly eccentric.

Building a folly to provide employment for local workmen, or a focal point for visitors to admire, may be a trifle odd but it doesn't count as truly eccentric.

Wearing flamboyant clothes (in the mode of Beau Brummel) or collecting vast quantities of something don't necessarily make an individual truly eccentric (though bibliomaniac Richard Heber makes it onto our list).

There are, of course, many notable eccentrics who didn't make it onto the list.

The most notable of those who missed selection was probably the composer Lord Berners. (He used the name Gerald Tyrwhitt when composing but later, when decomposing, reverted to Lord Berners.)

Lord Berners hated company when travelling by train and in order to have the carriage to himself he used to check his temperature anally every five minutes. He carried a large thermometer for this purpose. This usually had the desired effect quite quickly.

And the 18th century connoisseur, gardener, aesthete, bibliophile and patron of the arts William Beckford, also missed the cut, though his behaviour was certainly unusual from time to time. Beckford hated hunting so much that when he found a pack of hounds trespassing on his land he gave orders that a seven mile long and twelve foot high wall be immediately built around his house to make sure that it didn't happen again.

The real eccentric behaves in a way that seems to him to be entirely natural, logical and sensible. He doesn't do odd things occasionally. He doesn't sit in a bath of spaghetti to raise money for charity or push a bed up a mountain for a university rag day stunt. He doesn't simply wear flashy bowties or dye his hair. He doesn't have an unusual hobby (restoring steam trains or dredging canals) because his whole life is unusual. The true eccentric sees nothing odd in what he does or how he does it. His behaviour is, to him, perfectly rational.

In other words the true eccentric, a breed of men and women with whom England has always been exceptionally well-endowed, never thinks of him or herself as eccentric at all.

Here is the list of the top twelve English eccentrics of all time. You will note the people on the list are all men. This is not because of any sexist bias. It is because most eccentrics have been men. And you will note too that most of the people on our list were either rich or well-off. That is because when poor people behave in an eccentric way they are usually regarded as lunatics and locked up for their own protection. Sadly, only the wealthy can truly enjoy the delights of being genuinely eccentric. The wealthy can be eccentric in great style and (in the past, at least) their wealth frequently enabled them to ignore the law and escape the consequences. Maybe, eccentricity is simply one of the very few things that men do best.

1. John Mytton (1796-1834)

John Mytton's extraordinary adventures and eccentricities deserve a separate entry and so there is a separate Appendix devoted to him in this book. If eccentrics were rated with little dog heads instead of rosettes (to give an idea of their 'barking' rating) then Mytton would have five little dog heads beside his name. His eccentricity took him right to the edge of madness. But he wasn't mad. He was just completely barking. All other eccentrics must be measured against him.

2. Byron, George Gordon Noel, 6th Baron (1788-1824)

Famously described by one of his many mistresses as 'mad, bad and dangerous to know', Lord Byron was a poet and philanderer and is remembered as much for his life as for his work. He was a leading poet of the 19th century English Romantic movement and his poetry has been expertly described as irreverent, ironic, impudent, high-spirited, satirical, elegant, contemptuous, humorous, burlesque, unconventional, generous, humane and reckless. The same adjectives apply, equally accurately, to his life. Born with a deformed right foot which made him the butt of school boy jokes, his mother had mood swings which made him distrust women in later life. His father had died when he was just three-years-old, but not before managing to spend his mother's entire, considerable fortune. A female servant didn't help his attitude towards women. She took a succession of male lovers with the 9-year-old Byron as a spectator. At the age of 10, he became the 6th Baron, and with the title he inherited considerable estates. He attended Harrow School and discovered homosexuality. His mother began an affair with a 23-year-old rake, Lord Grey de Ruthyn who had made advances to the young Byron.

When he went to Cambridge in 1805, Byron patronised prostitutes with steadfast enthusiasm and fell in love with a choirboy called Edleston. When he put on weight, he played cricket wearing six waistcoats so that he would sweat and lose weight. While at the university he published his first poems (Hours of Idleness) and took his first mistress, a girl called Caroline whom he dressed, and passed off as, a boy. The reviews of his first book were poor and so in 1809 he published 'English Bards and Scotch Reviewers', a satirical poem attacking the major literary figures of the time. He then left London and started a tour of Greece, Albania, Turkey and Spain with a friend called Hobhouse who was writing a book called *Sodomy Simplified* (which, not surprisingly, never found a publisher). When Hobhouse abandoned him in Greece, Byron acquired a 15-year-old Greek boy called Nicolo and spent a good deal of money on prostitutes. He returned to England in 1812 and John Murray published 'Childe Harold's Pilgrimage'. The poem, inspired by his journey, describes the exploits of a world-weary young lord who tries everything when he is young and finds later life boring. Byron became an overnight celebrity. Young men imitated his brooding manner and his limp. Young women, attracted by his passion and his pleas for liberty and justice, threw themselves at him (though possibly not literally). Byron's new lovers included Lady Caroline Lamb and her mother-in-law Lady Melbourne.

When he returned to Cambridge, Byron began an incestuous affair with his half-sister Augusta. He was then seduced by a promiscuous woman called Lady Oxford. Byron and Augusta then moved to Newstead Abbey where she became pregnant. To silence the gossips Byron, by now aged 26, married Lady Melbourne's niece, a prim heiress called Annabelle. The marriage wasn't much of a success, possibly because Byron continued to 'flirt' with his half sister and possibly because he was nearly always drunk. When his wife became pregnant, he sodomised her late into her pregnancy. Exhausted by Byron's demands, by quarrels, and by giving birth, Annabelle ran away and went home. When her parents found out what had been going on they would not let her return to her wicked husband. Suddenly the great poet was unfashionable and unwanted. Byron quit England in 1816. Having sold Newstead Abbey for £94,500 he rented a palazzo in Venice where he initiated orgies which shocked even the previously un-shockable Venetians. Byron's home soon became pretty much a brothel. The man himself was now fat and balding though still in his early thirties. While in Italy he wrote Don Juan, a long, witty poem about a handsome, young man's adventures with women. A tempestuous affair with a married woman caused some problems and Byron left Italy in rather a rush. He became an enthusiastic supporter of Italian and Greek freedom fighters and joined a secret Italian nationalist society. In Greece he led troops against the Turks. While doing so he caught a fever and, in proper poetic fashion, died young at the age of 36. His family requested that he be buried in Westminster Abbey. Perhaps not entirely surprisingly, the request was refused.

3. Rev F.W.Densham (1870-1953)

When the Rev Densham was rector of the church in Warleggan, Cornwall, he painted the twelfth century church red and blue. The pillars were painted with black and white stripes. This decor didn't go down too well with the congregation. In his final year as rector, the Rev Densham conducted most of his services in an empty church (on one occasion there was just one person attending a service, on all other occasions the rector was alone). To keep himself company, the Rev Densham filled the church with cardboard cut-out figures and name cards and then delivered passionate sermons to his cardboard flock. Why didn't the parishioners go to church? Well, perhaps they were put off by the fact that if they turned up at all he would be incredibly rude to them. Or it might have been the fact that there was an eight foot high barbed wire fence around the rectory. Or perhaps they were put off by the fact that the rectory was bare of furniture and the rector lived on porridge and nettles. Saddest of all, behind the eight foot high fence, the garden was full of roundabouts and other games which the Rector had constructed for the local children. None ever visited and no one ever used the toys he made.

4. William John Cavendish Bentinck Scott, 5th Duke of Portland (1800-1879)

The Duke was mad keen on building things. He built pagodas, lakes, a skating rink and a huge stable for a string of race horses which never raced (or even ridden). He built the biggest indoor riding school in Europe. It was never used. He did however insist that all his staff learned to skate and skated regularly (whether they wanted to or not). His most remarkable building was an underground ballroom which was 174 feet long, and had a ceiling painted to represent a sunset and a thousand gas lights. He built an underground railway to connect his house to the ballroom but never used the ballroom. He also had fifteen miles of tunnel built under his estate so that he could move about without ever meeting anyone. Another underground railway enabled staff to take meals the 150 yards from the kitchen to the dining room. One of the tunnels was big enough for him to drive through in a coach and four. He loathed any sort of contact with people and when he had to travel he did so in a specially built coach which had low seats and blinds. He would be driven to the nearest station and the coach would be put onto a special flat car on the train. As well as the underground ballroom he also built an underground billiard room, big enough for twelve full sized tables, and several underground libraries. Like the ballroom these remained unused. All the underground rooms were painted pink. Many, like the rooms in the main house, had a plumbed in lavatory right in the middle of the room. At one point the Duke employed 15,000 workmen. Every one of them was given a donkey and an umbrella as a bonus and no one was ever sacked unless they acknowledged the duke's presence. Anyone who spoke to him, nodded, bowed, touched their cap or glanced in his direction would be fired on the spot. The duke wrote to his staff if he wanted to tell them to do something. He hated human contact so much that if he needed the doctor, he would make the physician wait outside the bedroom door and shout details of his symptoms through the door. He had a vast collection of wigs, false beards and false moustaches so that if he had to go out into the world he could do so without being recognised. However, since very few people knew what he looked like this was probably unnecessary. The duke gave away vast amounts of money to local charities and to poor families and despite his eccentricities was much loved.

5. George Hanger, later Baron Coleraine (1751-1824)

By the age of 22, George had married a gypsy, fought three duels, reached the rank of colonel and been wounded in the American War of Independence. He then retired to devote himself to gambling, drinking, racing and whoring. He wasn't terribly good as a gambler. He once bet £500 that 20 turkeys would beat twenty geese over a ten mile race course. He lost. He spent eighteen months in a debtors' prison and when he came out he went into business as a coal merchant.

6. Edward Wortley Montagu (1713-1776)

Montagu spent most of his life roaming around the Middle East, dressed in Turkish costume, but his eccentric life started before his travels. He ran away from Westminster School and exchanged places with a young sweep so that his disappearance wouldn't be noticed. After working as a chimney boy, he apprenticed himself to a fisherman and sold flounders in Rotherhithe. At the age of thirteen, he enrolled himself at Oxford University as a student of Oriental languages. He immediately seduced his landlady. He then dressed as a cabin boy and went to Portugal on board a merchant ship. In Portugal he became a mule driver. When eventually brought home, his parents sent him to the West Indies with a tutor. Montagu returned to London at the age of 17 and married a washerwoman. She was the first of many wives. He subsequently acquired additional wives in Egypt, Italy, Spain and elsewhere. In between marriage ceremonies, he became an army officer, a scholar in Oriental languages and MP for Huntingdon. In London, he wore an iron wig studded with diamonds (he changed the diamonds every day) and collected snuff boxes and debts. He had acquired another wife while visiting a highwayman in prison and with accusations of bigamy over his head he left the country again. At his first port of call, Alexandria, he met and eloped with the wife of the Danish consul, after falsely telling the woman that her husband had been drowned at sea. He wandered around the Middle East (papers relating his travels were read out at meetings of the Royal Society), put the Danish consul's wife into a nunnery and wandered off. He went back for her several years later (she was faithfully waiting for him) and married her. Things weren't perfect, however, and so Montagu changed his religion from Catholic to Moslem and married a black Egyptian serving girl. He ended up in Venice attended by a black African servant and two half naked eunuchs. He lived in a Venetian palazzo and flew the Turkish flag on his gondola. At this point his father died and Montagu discovered that in order to benefit financially he had to marry and have a son. So he put an advertisement in the London papers inviting genteel and pregnant women to apply to be his wife. Sadly, before he could travel back to London to select the winner (from a number of applicants) he died when a bone got stuck in his throat.

7. Richard Heber, (1774-1833)

Heber was born in Cheshire and by the time he was eight-years-old he had a sizeable library of his own, all properly catalogued. After his father died and he inherited the family fortune, he started collecting in earnest. He invariably bought three copies of any book he liked (one to store, one to read and one to lend) and filled two London houses, a house in Cheshire and houses in Paris, Brussels, Antwerp and Ghent with books. He would travel miles to buy a single book and in Paris once bought an entire library of 30,000 volumes in one go. In all his houses, the rooms, cupboards, passageways and corridors were choked with books.

8. George Osbaldeston (1786-1866)

George reckoned that any week in which he didn't spend six days in the saddle was a week wasted. His feats of sporting endurance are legendary. He once won a bet by galloping two hundred miles in under nine hours (he used 27 horses). At a ball in Lincoln he noticed one attractive woman admiring the orchid worn by another. The orchid wearer rudely snubbed the admiring woman and Osbaldeston was incensed. He leapt onto his horse and rode to a private conservatory 25 miles away where he bought the best orchid there. After four hours of hard riding he reappeared in the ballroom and presented the orchid to the snubbed woman. They reputedly danced until dawn though what happened then is not recorded.

9. Simon Ellerton (1695-1799)

Ellerton was a keen walker who often walked from Durham (where he lived) to London. He would happily do the journey to perform errands for the local gentry. While out walking one day, he picked up a stone for a cottage he was building. This soon became a habit and before long he had become accustomed to picking up one or two stones every time he went out. He would put them on his head to carry them, claiming eventually that he could walk more comfortably with a weight on his head than he could without. He carried on with this even after his cottage had been completed and until his death he always carried a heavy stone on his head when he left home. When asked why, he would explain that the stone was there to keep his hat on.

10. Thomas Gibson Bowles (known as Cap'en Tommy) (1842-1922)

Bowles was the founder and publisher of the magazines the *Lady* and *Vanity Fair*. When his wife died leaving him with four children under the age of 10, he decided to have his daughters clothed by the naval tailor who made clothes for his sons. As a result his two daughters, Sydney and Dorothy, wore thick, blue, serge naval uniforms and sailors' caps until they were seventeen. (Sydney would later become Lady Redesdale, the mother of the famous Mitford girls.) When the girls eventually managed to persuade their father that they should be dressed as young women, Bowles consulted an 'actress' friend. With her guidance, the girls were dressed in low-necked, black velvet gowns with red sashes. Bowles was MP for King's Lynn from 1892 to 1906 though in 1899 he announced to his daughter Dorothy, by then keeping home for him, that he was fed up with politics and intended to move to China. He told Dorothy to close up the house and pack. She did as she was told. All the furniture was covered in dustsheets and a caretaker hired to look after the house. She then sat outside the house, with the luggage, in a four wheeled carriage waiting for her father to join her. But as Bowles left the house, it started to rain. He lent into the cab and said: 'My dear child, it's raining. We won't go.'

11. Sir Thomas Barrett-Lennard (1857 to 1918)

Sir Thomas, the squire of Belhus in Essex, was a great animal lover. On muddy days, if he thought the going was too heavy for a horse to pull his carriage with him inside it, he would jump out and run alongside to save the horse the effort. He loved all animals, and his servants were instructed to keep a fresh bowl of water in the corn rick for the rats. When he saw a butcher mistreating a pony, he tore off his coat and thrashed the man. He cared about humans too. He would often answer his own front door to save his butler the trouble and dressed so scruffily that he was once given a tip for opening his park gates to a visiting carriage.

12. Francis Henry Egerton, eighth Earl of Bridgewater (1756-1829)

The Earl loved his dogs and treated them like dinner guests. With an annual income of £40,000 a year he could afford to do pretty much what he liked. At dinner the dogs sat on chairs dressed in fashionable finery. They had handmade leather shoes on their feet and linen napkins round their necks. A footman stood behind each dog. If a dog didn't behave properly it would suffer the indignity of being dressed in yellow servants' livery and sent to eat in the servants' hall for a week. When the dogs were taken for a walk, a servant with an umbrella would accompany them to make sure they didn't get wet. Lord Bridgewater also had a passion for boots. He wore a different pair each day, never wearing the same boots twice and so never having the joy of wearing a comfortable pair. Each night the boots he had taken off would be placed alongside the previous day's boots and by the time he died, the house was filled with rows and rows of boots. They were not cleaned so that he could find out what the weather had been like simply by finding the boots for that day. His boots were his diary. Egerton lived in France for 30 years but never learned French. In later years he used to entertain guests by ordering his secretary to read out extracts from a long and constantly changing will. In the gardens of his Paris home he kept 300 rabbits, 300 pigeons and 300 partridges. The birds had their wings clipped. This menagerie enabled him to wander into his garden and shoot his dinner when the fancy took him. When he travelled he never did so lightly. Packing would take months. On one occasion he set off followed by sixteen carriages laden with luggage. He returned home hours after setting off having abandoned his trip after an unsatisfactory lunch at an inn. When he died each servant received a mourning suit, a cocked hat and three pairs of worsted stockings. A monument on his grave depicts a woman with a stork behind her, an elephant by her side and dolphin at her feet. Needless to say Egerton designed the monument himself.

(This list is adapted from *England's Glory* written by Vernon Coleman and Donna Antoinette Coleman – now sadly out of print.)

Appendix 5: Mad Jack Mytton

John Mytton (1796-1834) was the most eccentric Englishman of all time. (And he had a good deal of competition.)

Mytton crammed a good deal into his short life and was described by his family as 'high spirited'.

Here are two dozen examples of his high-spirited nature.

1. He was asked to leave Westminster School after a year for 'fighting with the masters'. He then went to Harrow where he lasted three days. After that he was taught at home by a series of tutors. He treated these to a series of practical jokes – including leaving a horse in one tutor's bedroom.

2. When it was decided that he should attend Cambridge University, he arranged for 2,000 bottles of port to be ready for his arrival. In the end, he changed his mind and didn't go to Cambridge. There is no record of what happened to the port.

3. On his 21st birthday, Mytton inherited £60,000 and vast estates. However, in the remaining 17 years of his life he got through more than £500,000 and ended up bankrupt.

4. He spent a year in the 7th Hussars. Most of the time he was gambling, drinking and racing horses. At a farewell dinner he persuaded his horse, Baronet, to leap the fully laden mess table.

5. In 1819, Mytton decided to seek election as MP for Shrewsbury. While campaigning, he walked round the constituency with £10 notes pinned to his hat. As the notes were taken so they were replaced. Mytton spent £10,000 in this way and won the election by 384 votes to 287.

6. When Mytton got to the House of Commons, he found the first debate he attended uninteresting. He left and never went back.

7. Every morning, Mytton drank five bottles of port before lunch. If the port ran out (not something that happened often) he would drink eau-de-Cologne or lavender water.

8. Mytton liked to drive his gig into rabbit holes at high speed to see if it would turn over. (It invariably did.) When a passenger complained that his carriage driving was reckless and might overturn the carriage, Mytton scoffed and said: 'What? Never been upset in a gig? What a damned slow fellow you must have been all your life.' He then deliberately ran the carriage up a steep incline and overturned it so that the passenger could experience an 'upset'.

9. Mytton kept 60 cats which he dressed in liveries suitable to their breeds. He was even fonder of dogs and had 2,000 of those. When his favourite dog Tizer was losing a fight with a friend's dog, Mytton bit the other dog's nose and held on until the dog gave in. Some of the dogs were fed on steak and champagne. His favourite horse, called Baronet, was allowed to wander throughout Halston Hall and would lie with Mytton in front of the fire drinking mulled port.

10. On one occasion, Mytton rode into his dining room in full hunting costume. To the alarm of his guests he was riding his pet brown bear called Nell at the time. When Mytton dug his spurs in, the bear bit him on the leg.

11. In 1826, he rode a horse into the Bedford Hotel in Leamington Spa. He rode the horse up the grand staircase and out onto the balcony. He then jumped the horse over the diners seated in the restaurant below before leaping through the window and into the Parade, the main town's main street. He remained seated on his horse throughout, and won the bet.

12. Mytton once replaced the last few pages of the local vicar's sermon with pages from the *Sporting Magazine*.

13. He once got his horse dealer drunk and put him to bed with two bull terriers and Nell, the brown bear. Mytton sent the same horse dealer to a banker in Shrewsbury, ostensibly to collect money for him. He gave the dealer a note to hand to the banker, who was also a governor of the local mental hospital. The note read: 'Sir, please admit the bearer, George Underhill, to the lunatic asylum. Your obedient servant, John Mytton.'

14. When a tough Welsh miner tried to head off his hounds, Mytton leapt off his horse and challenged the man to a fistfight. After twenty rounds the miner gave in. Mytton congratulated the man and gave him half a sovereign.

15. When his creditors became a little too aggressive, Mytton moved to France. In a hotel in Calais he developed hiccups and decided to get rid of the problem by giving himself a fright. He set fire to his nightshirt. This cured the hiccups ('The hiccup is gone, by God!' he is reputed to have said.) but he was badly burned. Advised to stay in bed for a month he arranged to go out for dinner. But when his dining companion sent a two horse equipage for him, Mytton, covered in bandages, refused to get into it, claiming that he would sooner walk than ride in a carriage with less than four horses. Supported by two servants, he walked a mile and a half to dinner.

16. After being released from debtors' prison in 1832, Mytton met a pretty, young woman on Westminster Bridge. (Mytton's wife Caroline had run away two years earlier.) Mytton had never met the girl before but asked her name and where she was going. She said her name was Susan and she didn't know where she was going. Mytton then offered her £500 a year to live with him. She accepted and spent the next two years living with him in Calais. She was with him when he died.

17. On separate occasions, Mytton fought both dogs and bears armed with nothing more than his teeth.

18. In winter he went duck hunting in his night shirt or, on occasion, completely naked – just to make things more exciting.

19. He invented a game which involved chasing rats across a frozen pond while wearing skates.

20. He bet a friend that he could give him a fifteen minute start and still beat him home. Mytton won easily by taking a short cut through a lake which he forced his horse to swim knowing that if he had been thrown from his horse he would have drowned because he could not swim.

21. When out riding in bad weather, Mytton would knock on a cottage door and ask if his horse could dry off by the fire. Since he owned most of the local cottages he was never refused.

22. His wardrobe contained 700 pairs of boots, 150 pairs of riding breeches, 1,000 hats and nearly 3,000 shirts.

23. He died, in prison, from alcohol poisoning. He was just 38-years-old. More than 3,000 friends and acquaintances attended his funeral.

24. For some undisclosed reason, John Mytton was known to his friends as 'Mad Jack'.

(This list is adapted from *England's Glory* by Vernon Coleman and Donna Antoinette Coleman.)

Appendix 6: Lady Hillingdon's Confession

The well-known saying 'lie back and think of England' (said to be favoured by ladies of breeding who regard sex as nothing more than an event necessary to keep England well populated with the 'right sort of people') originated with a woman called Lady Hillingdon.

Here is the relevant quote from her diary:

'I am happy now that Charles calls on my bedchamber less frequently than of old. As it is, I now endure but two calls a week and when I hear his steps outside my door I lie down on my bed, close my eyes, open my legs and think of England.' – Lady Hillingdon in her Journal for 1912

Charles William Mills, later the 2nd Baron Hillingdon, was a banker and politician who sat in the House of Commons at the end of the 19th century. He married Alice Marion Harbord in 1886 and became the baron when his father died in 1898.

The Author

Vernon Coleman is an author and doctor. This is the 15th book about Bilbury – all in 'The Young Country Doctor' series. His novels include the series about Mrs Caldicot. The titles in that series are: *Mrs Caldicot's Cabbage War*, *Mrs Caldicot's Knickerbocker Glory*, *Mrs Caldicot's Easter Parade* and *Mrs Caldicot's Turkish Delight*. Individual novels include: *Mr Henry Mulligan, The Truth Kills, Second Chance, Paris in my Springtime, It's Never Too Late, The Hotel Doctor, My Secret Years with Elvis'* and many others. All of these books are available as ebooks on Amazon. All the books in 'The Young Country Doctor' series are available as ebooks on Amazon.

Before you go…

Thank you for your company. Sorry to go on about it, and apologies if you already have done so, but if you have enjoyed this volume in The Young Country Doctor series, I really would be very grateful if you would spare a moment to write a short review.
Thank you
Vernon Coleman

Made in the USA
Middletown, DE
25 April 2021